The Complete Meal Prep Instant Pot Cookbook for Beginners #2019-20

Simple, Easy and Healthy Instant Pot Recipes for Smart People

LOSE UP TO 20 POUNDS IN 21 DAYS

Jessica Smith

CONTENTS

BEEF AND PORK...80

DESSERT RECIPES 95

21-DAY MEAL PLAN TO LOSE 20 POUNDS 107

INTRODUCTION

Have you ever had a feeling that your life has become dominated by activities revolving around working and organizing food? A typical week consisting of waking up in the morning, rushing to work, commuting, working, hasty lunch break, commuting home, eating dinner, and running errands, and you quickly notice there's not much time left for anything else.

And what about money flowing out of your wallet to satisfy your food whims?

Can't resist buying from a burger stand or dropping into a bakery for a croissant? The world doesn't end if you do so once in a while, but if added up, you may quickly realize you are spending lots of money on stuff you could easily do without.

We may argue that's just the way life is or not, but one thing is sure. It does not take much to make it way better. Planning meals in an organized way for the whole week (or more) may sound like a big-time investment, but in reality, it saves us a lot of time and money.

How much happier would your family, partner, or friends then be? How much would you develop yourself, having more time to follow a passion or hobby? How much more money would there be left in your pocket if you stopped spending it randomly whenever you have a whim.

If you start wondering if a conventional cookbook could offer you so much, the answer is NO. Not a conventional one. But this one – YES!

Whether we like it or not, our world is accelerating. This book is a culinary response to that acceleration.

MEAL PREP: WHAT IT REALLY IS?

A solution in the era of a constant rush.

In broad outline, Meal Prepping is preparing multiple meals at the same time, ahead of time. It's a method that helps you save time by cooking meals for other days of the week, or even month, up front. The more the better, within reason, of course.

This system is not only meant to give you more free time and save money, but it's also a perfect way to master multitasking skills and maximize the time spent in the kitchen.

Some people believe the more they have to do, the more efficient they become with getting it done. In this method, that rule works perfectly. Don't be surprised if your efficiency reaches new dimensions.

WHAT ARE THE BENEFITS FOR YOU?

More time to spend doing better things.

I bet you often wish you could pay to have more free time. We like to think about everything short-term. Thirty minutes, an hour, or maybe even hours per week may not sound that convincing to you. How about dozens of hours per month? Hundreds per year? Does it change the perspective now?

Eat clean. No room for junk food anymore.

Through organizing your meals, you greatly decrease the risk of snacking on unhealthy, processed food from packages and fast foods prevalent at every corner of the city.

Having prepared proportions, you quickly notice that even if you fancy

some grab-and-go tacos or a burger, you will not go for it. Getting food from vending machines will also become a thing of the past because it means having your pre-prepared lunch or dinner filling your stomach up. And, of course, you would not throw out something you spent time and money on.

You will realize quickly that meal prepping makes you a healthier person. When you eat cleaner, you feel better, not only because you have a sense of control over your life, but also because this type of food event, though often irresistible, is a happiness killer. Think of the food as your fuel and of yourself as a top class luxurious car. Would you fuel it with low-quality gas that could damage the engine? Probably not. Meal prepping forces you to skip low-quality fuel and treat your engine better.

From planning meals to planning life.

A great side effect of meal prepping is that you learn how to organize life better.

Is it not a common a thing to waste those little windows of time we have between particular cooking activities? Think how much more you could get done if only you knew how and if you had a good method to do so.

Another aspect is that you have to plan your shopping carefully. If you have never used shopping lists before, it's perhaps time to start. Based on that, you may adjust meals and portions accordingly. You will learn how to prepare and eat just enough without having leftovers or overeating. If you prepare meals for the whole family, you will save yourself the trouble of preparing different food every day and then cleaning it all up.

It develops you as a person because once mastered, that skill may go beyond cooking and will surely help you organize your life better.

Weight loss becomes easier.

Now, as you have the whole-day schedule prepared, you are less likely to snack outside the schedule. Having a general plan for anything in life strongly builds a sense of discipline.

Therefore, if you combine meal prepping with the knowledge of your body and nutrition, you will create an excellent lifestyle where weight loss is not a goal itself, but merely a means to an end. You will not have to obsessively focus on counting

Calories every time you're thinking of eating something you have not planned.

Losing weight happens automatically as a side effect of eating appropriate, schedule- based meals.

Nutritional education.

If you want to become an excellent meal planner, some of the basic knowledge about food will come in very handy. Knowing how to compose a balanced meal is not that difficult. A proper content of proteins, fats, and carbohydrates in an adequate ratio will help you remain satiated for a longer period of time. As a result, hunger pangs will diminish and you will stop snacking on foods your body doesn't really need.

You may not only develop a genuine interest in healthy eating habits, but you will also be challenged to learn how to pack and store things properly. Simple as it sounds, a bit of know-how is necessary.

Last but not least, labelling pre-prepared meals will keep your food organized and make sure you have control over the freshness. Meal prepping does not mean eating stale food.

TOP TIPS FOR A GOOD START

1. ### PLAN AHEAD. PICK A DAY AND STICK TO IT.

   Sundays are considered the best day to prepare for the whole week.
   Draw up a list of meals and days and keep it on paper. You can easily print meal planners from the internet, which may be an excellent solution here.
   Better yet, learn to plan two or even three weeks ahead.

2. ### GO FOR DIVERSITY

   That means not repeating the same dish seven times a week. Prepare two to three alternatives to use on different days if you do not want to experience nutritional burn-out. It may be something as simple as changing the source of proteins (i.e. meat for fish or tofu), rice for pasta, or a different type of vegetables.

3. ### MAKE A LIST BEFORE GOING SHOPPING

   This will train you to stick to the plan, not toss impulse items into your trolley. You will save money and time and keep yourself from buying junk food. If something's not available in your fridge, you will not eat it.

4. ### KEEP IT SIMPLE

   Although trying more difficult recipes is most welcome, I recommend for the beginning sticking to simple recipes. Over time, as you become more adept, you may increase the complexity or try your own recipes.

5. ### COOK MORE ITEMS AT ONCE, WHENEVER POSSIBLE.

   A good example of that would be roasting a couple of things in the oven or on the stove. It's not only time saving, but your electricity bill will look way better.

6. INVEST IN GOOD-QUALITY CONTAINERS AND MASON JARS.

These will help you store things longer without risk of wasting food, and they look fancy. Eating from such containers makes things taste better.
I would also recommend buying larger pots and frying pans

7. BUY PRE-CUT VEGETABLES

Even though they may be a bit more expensive, they make your life easier and may save you some additional time.

8. DRINK LOTS OF WATER

It may sound really obvious, but very often we confuse hunger pangs with dehydration. Water fills your stomach and you do not feel hunger, which makes it a real basis for each diet.

9. EMPLOY COOKING DEVICES LIKE SLOW COOKER.

THINGS TO AVOID:

- Processed, packaged foods like pasta, cheese, pizzas
- Processed, packaged meat
- Vegetable oils
- Sugary beverages
- All kinds of cookies, cakes, and pastries
- Candy bars
- All kinds of fast foods, including French Fries
- White bread made of processed white wheat-flour
- Most fruit juices as they contain tons of sugar
- Potato chips
- Margarine
- Energy drinks
- Ice creams

All things are difficult before they become easy.

The concept of meal prepping is to maintain a healthy lifestyle in a rushing environment. The idea offers the wisdom of not taking the easy way out and eating junk food tempting us everywhere we go. Instead, we learn to take responsibility for what we eat and what we become as a result.

These recipes are meant to help you initiate the changes and go through the tough beginning. But the results are well worth the time.

This book is an investment that pays huge interests quickly without forcing you to spend a lot of money first.

Its success is entirely dependent on your determination in sticking to the plan and giving up things you considered normal before.

Recipes in the book are predominantly easy and perfect for beginners. Advanced cooking freaks will definitely find something for themselves as well.

Buddha said, "To enjoy good health, to bring true happiness to one's family, to bring peace to all, one must first discipline and control one's own mind." This could not be truer. In order to take any action, we first need to realize the importance of our diet and how it affects the temples our bodies are. Love the life you have while enjoying the journey to a better, healthier life.

BREAKFAST AND BRUNCH

Fruity Pecan Breakfast Cobbler

Preparation time: 10 minutes | Cooking time: 15 minutes | Servings: 4

Ingredients

½ cup Pecan Halves

2 Pears, peeled and diced

2 Apples, peeled and diced

2 Plums, pitted and diced

4 tbsp Honey

4 tbsp Sunflower Seeds

4 tbsp Coconut Oil or Butter

½ tsp Cinnamon

½ cup Shredded Coconut, unsweetened

Instructions

Combine the fruits, honey, and coconut oil in the Instant Pot. Stir to combine. Put the lid on and turn it clockwise to close. You will know it is sealed once you hear the chime. Press "STEAM" and set the cooking time to 10 minutes.

When you hear the beeping, release the pressure quickly. Open the lid and transfer the fruits to a bowl.

Add the remaining ingredients to the Instant Pot and stir with the cooking liquid to combine. Set to "STEAM" again and cook for an additional 5 minutes. Stir in the fruit mixture.

Storing

Let the mixture cool completely and divide between 4 airtight containers. Place in the fridge for 4-5 days. To freeze, transfer to 4 Ziploc bags and freeze up to 3 months.

Nutrition facts per serving

Calories 450, Protein 4g, Total Carbs 45g, Fat 32.4g, Fiber 7g

Mini Bacon Quiches

Preparation time: 10 minutes | Cooking time: 15 minutes | Servings: 4

Ingredients

8 Eggs
8 Bacon Slices, cooked and crumbled
½ Red Onion, diced
1 Bell Pepper, diced
3 cups Water

Instructions

Pour half the water into your Instant Pot and lower the trivet. Beat the eggs in a bowl and stir in the onion, bacon, and pepper. Divide the mixture between 8 silicone muffin cups. Arrange half of the muffin cups on top of the trivet.

Put the lid on and turn it clockwise to close. You will know it is sealed once you hear the chime. Press "MANUAL" and set the cooking time to 8 minutes by pressing the "+" and "-" buttons.

When you hear the beeping, press "KEEP WARM/CANCEL" to turn the Instant Pot off. Release the pressure quickly by moving the pressure release handle from "Sealing" to "Venting". Make sure to keep your hands away from the steam to avoid burning. Open the lid and remove the muffin cups.

Pour the rest of the water inside and arrange the remaining muffin cups on the trivet. Close the lid again and cook for additional 8 minutes on HIGH. Again, do a quick pressure release.

Storing

Place the leftovers in an airtight container and refrigerate for up to 3 days. For freezing, place 2 of the quiches in a Ziploc bag. Let them thaw overnight in the fridge and then microwave for a couple of minutes.

Nutrition facts per serving

Calories 236, Protein 20g, Total Carbs 2.2g, Fat 16g, Fiber 0.5g

Mexican Salad

Preparation time: 10 minutes | Cooking time: 10 minutes | Servings: 4

Ingredients

2 cups Cannellini Beans, soaked overnight

1 tbsp Cumin

¼ tsp Chili Powder

½ cup chopped Cilantro

2 tbsp Vinegar

½ cup Olive Oil

4 ½ cups Water

1 cup chopped Red Onions

1 tsp minced Garlic

1 Cup diced Tomatoes

1 cup canned Corn

Instructions

Combine the beans and water in the Instant Pot. Put the lid on and turn it clockwise to seal. After the chime, select the "MANUAL" cooking mode and set the cooking time to 20 minutes. Cook on HIGH.

When the timer goes off, press the "CANCEL" button. Move the handle to "Venting" to release the pressure quickly. When the pressure is fully released, open the lid.

Drain the beans and transfer to a large bowl. Add the rest of the ingredients and stir well to combine.

Storing

Divide the salad between 4 airtight containers. Place in the fridge and consume within 3-4 days. To freeze, divide among 4 Ziploc bags and place in the freezer. Consume within 3 months. Defrost in the fridge overnight and enjoy chilled.

Nutrition facts per serving

Calories 544, Protein 22g, Total Carbs 65g, Fat 26g, Fiber 15g

Bacon and Feta Couscous

Preparation time: 10 minutes | Cooking time: 10 minutes | Servings: 4

Ingredients

8 ounces Couscous

4 Bacon slices, diced

1 cup crumbled Feta Cheese

2 tbsp Tomato Paste

1 tbsp Butter

1 ¼ cup Chicken Broth

Instructions

Press the "SAUTE" key and add the butter to the Instant Pot. When melted, add the bacon and cook until crispy.

Add the couscous and cook for one more minute. Stir in the tomato paste and broth and close the lid. Turn clockwise, and when sealed, select "MANUAL". Set the cooking temperature to 5 minutes. Cook on HIGH pressure.

When you hear the beeping, press "KEEP WARM/CANCEL" to turn the Instant Pot off. Release the pressure quickly by moving the pressure release handle from "Sealing" to "Venting". Make sure to keep your hands away from the steam to avoid burning. Open the lid and stir in the feta cheese and season with some salt and pepper. Let cool completely.

Storing

Transfer to 4 airtight containers and place in the fridge. You can use them for up to 3 days. To freeze, divide among 4 Ziploc bags and place in the freezer for up to 3 months. Defrost in microwave and heat for a few minutes to enjoy warm.

Nutrition facts per serving

Calories 300, Protein 17g, Total Carbs 36g, Fat 12g, Fiber 8g

Mashed Potatoes with Sausage and Cheese

Preparation time: 10 minutes | Cooking time: 15 minutes | Servings: 6

Ingredients

6 large Potatoes, cut into cubes

1 cup Warm Milk

¼ cup melted Butter

Pinch of Nutmeg

Salt and Pepper, to taste

1 cup Water

1 cup shredded Cheddar Cheese

1 pound Sausages, chopped

½ Onion, diced

1 tbsp Olive Oil

Instructions

Turn the Instant Pot on and set it to "SAUTE" Add the oil and heat until sizzling. Add the onions and cook for about 3 minutes.

When they become translucent, add the sausage. Cook for about 4 minutes or until crispy around the edges. Transfer the sausage and onions to a plate.

Combine the potatoes and water in the Instant Pot. Close the lid and turn clockwise to seal. Select "MANUAL" after the sealing chime sounds and set the cooking time to 5 minutes. Cook on HIGH pressure.

When you hear the beeping sound, press "KEEP WARM/CANCEL" to turn the Instant Pot off. Release the pressure quickly by moving the pressure release handle from "Sealing" to "Venting". Make sure to keep your hands away from the steam to avoid burning.

Open the lid, drain the potatoes, and transfer to a bowl. Mash the potatoes with a potato masher and stir in the milk, nutmeg, and season with salt and pepper.

Wipe the Instant Pot clean and add the mashed potatoes. Return the sausage and onion mixture as well. Stir in the cheese. Click the "SAUTE" button and cook with the lid off until the cheese is melted.

Allow to cool completely.

Storing

When cooled, divide among 6 airtight containers and place in the fridge. You can use them for up to 3 days. To freeze, divide among 6 Ziploc bags and place in the freezer for up to 3 months. Defrost in microwave and heat for a few minutes.

Nutrition facts per serving

Calories 430, Protein 20g, Total Carbs 39g, Fat 20g, Fiber 5g

Classic Mac & Cheese

Preparation time: 5 minutes | Cooking time: 7 minutes | Servings: 6

Ingredients

3 ½ cups Macaroni
1 ½ cups shredded Mozzarella Cheese
2 cups Heavy Cream
2 cups Stock
¼ cup Milk
2 tbsp Butter
Pinch of Nutmeg
1 ½ cups shredded Swiss Cheese

Instructions

Combine the stock and heavy cream in the Instant Pot. Add the macaroni and season with some salt and pepper. Put the lid on and turn clockwise to seal. Select "MANUAL" after the sealing chime sounds and set the cooking time to 7 minutes. Cook on HIGH pressure.

When you hear the beeping sound, release the pressure quickly. Open the lid and stir in the remaining ingredients. Let the macaroni cool completely.

Storing

When cooled, divide among 6 airtight containers and place in the fridge for up to 3 days. To freeze, divide among 6 Ziploc bags and place in the freezer for up to 3 months.

Nutrition facts per serving

Calories 570, Protein 17g, Total Carbs 40g, Fat 28g, Fiber 3g

Sausage, Spinach, and Onion Casserole

Preparation time: 10 minutes | Cooking time: 30 minutes | Servings: 6

Ingredients

2 tbsp Butter

10 Eggs

12 ounces cooked Sausage, diced

1 ½ cups chopped Spinach

1 Red Onion, diced

2 Potatoes, peeled and shredded

¼ tsp Garlic Powder

¼ tsp Turmeric Powder

1 ½ cups Water

Instructions

Grease a baking dish with cooking spray. Beat the eggs along with the garlic powder and turmeric. Stir in the potatoes, spinach, and sausage.

Set your pot to "SAUTE" and melt the butter. Cook the onion until soft, a few minutes. Stir in the egg mixture. Pour the egg mixture into the baking dish. Add water to the pot and lower the trivet. Place the baking dish on top. Put the lid on and turn it clockwise to close. Press "MANUAL" and set the cooking time to 25 minutes.

When you hear the beeping, release the pressure quickly. Open the lid and remove the baking dish from the Instant Pot. Let cool completely.

Storing

Slice the egg casserole into 6 equal pieces and divide between airtight containers. Place in the fridge for up to 3 days. To freeze, transfer to 6 Ziploc bags and freeze up to 3 months.

Nutrition facts per serving

Calories 425, Protein 24g, Total Carbs 13g, Fat 30g, Fiber

Beet Borscht

Preparation time: 10 minutes | Cooking time: 52 minutes | Servings: 8

Ingredients

1 tsp minced Garlic
1 Onion, diced
2 Celery Stalks, chopped
2 Carrots, sliced
1 tbsp chopped Parsley
8 cups diced Beets
3 cups shredded Cabbage
8 cups diced Beets

Instructions

Combine the broth and beets in the Instant Pot. Put the lid on and turn clockwise to seal. When you hear the chime, select the "MANUAL" cooking mode and set the time to 7 minutes. Cook on HIGH.

Turn the Instant Pot off by pressing "KEEP WARM / CANCEL" after the beep. Do a quick pressure release by moving the handle to "Venting".

Open the lid and add the remaining ingredients. Stir to combine and close the lid again. Set the Instant Pot to "SOUP" and the cooking time to 45 minutes.

After the beep, allow the pressure to come down naturally. Open the lid when the valve drops.

Let cool completely before storing.

Storing

When cooled, divide between 4 airtight containers (2 servings per container). Place in the fridge and consume within 3 days. To freeze transfer to a container and place in the freezer until just set. Divide between 4 Ziploc bags (2 servings per bag) and arrange them in a single layer until frozen. Consume within 3 months. Defrost in the microwave and heat for a few minutes to enjoy warm.

Nutrition facts per serving

Calories 110, Protein 4g, Total Carbs 24g, Fat 2g, Fiber 5g

Brie and Bacon Frittata

Preparation time: 10 minutes | Cooking time: 20 minutes | Servings: 6

Ingredients

8 Eggs, beaten
8 Bacon Slices
4 ounces Brie, diced
½ cup Heavy Cream
Salt and Pepper, to taste
1 ½ cup of Water

Instructions

Set the Instant Pot to "SAUTE" and add the bacon. Cook until it becomes crispy and transfer to a paper towel to drain the excess grease. Pour the water into the Instant Pot and lower the heat. Grease a baking dish with some cooking spray and set aside.

Mix eggs with the heavy cream and some salt and pepper. Crumble the cooked bacon inside and stir in the brie. Pour the mixture into the prepared dish.

Place the dish on top of the trivet. Put the lid on and turn it clockwise to close. You will know it is sealed once you hear the chime. Press "MANUAL" and cook on HIGH for 20 minutes.

When the timer goes off, press "CANCEL" to turn the Instant Pot off. Release the pressure naturally by letting the valve drop on its own. Open the lid and remove the dish form the Instant Pot. Let cool completely.

Storing

When cooled, slice the frittata into 6 equal pieces and place each of them in an air-tight container or in a Ziploc bag; put in the fridge. It is best to enjoy the frittata for up to 3 days. For freezing, divide between Ziploc bags and place in the freezer.

Nutrition facts per serving

Calories 210, Protein 13g, Total Carbs 3g, Fat 19g, Fiber 0g

Mexican Breakfast Casserole

Preparation time: 10 minutes | Cooking time: 26 minutes | Servings: 8

Ingredients

8 Eggs, beaten
1 cup shredded Mozzarella Cheese
½ Onion, chopped
½ cup Flour
1 pound Sausage
1 can Black Beans, drained
1 Bell Pepper, diced
½ cup sliced Green Onions
1 ½ cups Water

Instructions

Set the Instant Pot to "SAUTE" and place the sausage inside. Cook until browned while breaking it with a spatula. Add onions and cook for 2 more minutes. Transfer to a bowl.

In another bowl, whisk together the eggs and flour until no lumps are visible. Add the sausage mixture, black beans, pepper, green onions, and mozzarella. Stir to combine. Grease baking dish with some cooking spray and pour the egg mixture into it.

Pour the water into the Instant Pot, lower the rack, and place the baking dish on the rack. Put the lid on and turn it clockwise to close. You will know it is sealed once you hear the chime. Press "MANUAL" and cook on HIGH for 20 minutes.

When you hear the beeping, allow the pressure valve to come down on its own. Open the lid and remove the dish from the Instant Pot. Let cool on its own.

Storing

When cooled, slice the casserole into 8 pieces and place each in an airtight container and in the fridge. It is best to enjoy for up to 3 days. To freeze, place each piece into a Ziploc bag and in the freezer for up to 3 months.

Nutrition facts per serving

Calories 280, Protein 18g, Total Carbs 19g, Fat 18g, Fiber 4g

Potato and Sausage Egg Pie

Preparation time: 15 minutes | Cooking time: 20 minutes | Servings: 6

Ingredients

8 Eggs, beaten

1 tsp Garlic Powder

2 cups boiled and mashed Potatoes

1 Onion, diced

1 pound Pork Sausage

1 ½ cups Water

Instructions

Set your Instant Pot to "SAUTE" and add cook the sausage until browned. Grease a baking dish. Add in the cooked sausage, eggs, garlic powder, mashed potatoes, pepper, and onion. Stir well to combine.

Pour the water into the Instant Pot and lower the trivet. Place the baking dish on top of it. Put the lid on and turn it clockwise to close. Press "MANUAL" and cook on HIGH for 18 minutes.

When you hear the beeping sound, release the pressure quickly by moving the pressure release handle from "Sealing" to "Venting". Open the lid and remove the dish from the Instant Pot. Let cool completely.

Storing

When cooled, slice the pie into 6 pieces and place airtight containers and in the fridge. It is best to enjoy within the next 3 days. To freeze, divide between 6 Ziploc bags and place in the freeze. They will be good to enjoy for up to 2-3 months.

Nutrition facts per serving

Calories 353, Protein 22g, Total Carbs 6.5g, Fat 26g, Fiber 1.4g

Trout Salad

Preparation time: 10 minutes | Cooking time: 5 minutes | Servings: 6

Ingredients

1 Red Onion, sliced
1 Cucumber, sliced
1 cup Stock
1 tbsp Olive Oil
1 ½ cups chopped Tomatoes
2 cups chopped Lettuce
8 ounces Trout
1 tbsp chopped Parsley
Salt and Pepper, to taste
1 tbsp Lemon Juice

Instructions

Pour the stock into the Instant Pot. Season the trout with some salt and pepper and place in the steamer basket. Lower the basket into the pot and put the lid on. Seal by turning it clockwise. After you hear the chime, select "MANUAL" and set the cooking time for 5 minutes. Cook on HIGH.

When you hear the beeping, release the pressure quickly Open the lid and transfer the trout to a cutting board. When cooled, chop into small pieces.

Place all the remaining ingredients in a bowl and toss to combine. Top with the trout.

Storing

Divide the salad between 6 airtight containers and put in the fridge. You can use them for up to 3 days. To freeze, divide between 6 Ziploc bags or airtight containers and place in the freezer for up to 3 months. Defrost in the fridge and enjoy cold.

Nutrition facts per serving

Calories 140, Protein 12g, Total Carbs 5g, Fat 7g, Fiber 1g

Cheesy Almond Tuna Breakfast

Preparation time: 5 minutes | Cooking time: 5 minutes | Servings: 4

Ingredients

1 cup shredded Cheddar Cheese

2 cans Tuna, drained

1 tsp Garlic Powder

2 tbsp Butter

1 cup shaved Almonds

Instructions

Set the Instant Pot to "SAUTE" and place the butter inside. When melted, add the cheddar, tuna, and almonds. You will not be bringing the pot to pressure, so you don't need water. Cook on "SAUTE" with the lid off for 3 minutes. Allow to cool completely before storing.

Storing

When cooled, divide between 4 airtight containers and place in the fridge. You can enjoy the tuna for up to 3 days. Just heat it in the microwave and voila.

To freeze, divide among 6 Ziploc bags and place in the freezer for up to 3 months. Defrost in microwave and heat for a few minutes.

Nutrition facts per serving

Calories 150, Protein 10g, Total Carbs 6g, Fat 5g, Fiber 2g

Prosciutto Omelet with Carrots and Potatoes

Preparation time: 10 minutes | Cooking time: 9 minutes | Servings: 4

Ingredients

2 Carrots, shredded

8 Eggs, beaten

½ cup Milk or Almond Milk

2 cups shredded Sweet Potatoes

5 Prosciutto Slices, diced

Salt and Pepper, to taste

Instructions

Set the Instant Pot to "SAUTE" and cook the prosciutto until crispy. Arrange the potatoes on top. Top with the carrots.

In a bowl mix in the eggs with the milk, season with salt and pepper, and pour this mixture over the carrots. Put the lid on and turn it clockwise to close. Press "MANUAL" and set the cooking time to 7 minutes. When you hear the beeping, release the pressure quickly. Open the lid and let the omelet cool completely.

Storing

When cooled, slice the omelet into 4. Divide between airtight containers or Ziploc bags and refrigerate for up to 3 days. To freeze, transfer to 4 Ziploc bags and freeze up to 3 months.

Nutrition facts per serving

Calories 270, Protein 18g, Total Carbs 17g, Fat 14g, Fiber 2g

Chocolate Quinoa

Preparation time: 3 minutes | Cooking time: 1 minutes | Servings: 4

Ingredients

1 cup Quinoa   2 tbsp Honey
1 tsp Cocoa Powder   ½ tsp Vanilla Extract
2 tbsp Chocolate Chips   1 ½ cups Water

Instructions

Place all the ingredients in your Instant Pot and stir to combine. Put the lid on and turn it clockwise to close. Press "MANUAL" and cook on HIGH for 1 minutes.

After the beep, wait for about 10 minutes before releasing the pressure quickly. Open the lid and let the quinoa cool completely.

Storing

When cooled, divide between 4 airtight containers and place in the fridge for up to 4-6 days. To freeze, place in a container and into the freezer for up to 3-6 months.

Nutrition facts per serving

Calories 205, Protein 6g, Total Carbs 41g, Fat 3g, Fiber 0g

Alfredo Pizza

Preparation time: 10 minutes | Cooking time: 5 minutes | Servings: 2

Ingredients

1 Pizza Dough
1 ½ cups Water
¼ cup Alfredo Sauce
½ cup shredded Mozzarella Cheese
¼ tsp dried Oregano

Instructions

Line a baking dish that fits in the Instant Pot and set aside. Roll out the pizza dough on a flat, floured surface. Transfer to the lined baking dish. Spread the Alfredo sauce over and top with the cheese. Sprinkle with the oregano.

Pour the water into the Instant Pot and lower the trivet. Place the dish on top of the trivet and close the lid by turning clockwise. After the chime, select the "MANUAL" cooking mode and set the cooking time to 5 minutes. Cook on HIGH.

When the timer goes off, release the pressure quickly. Remove the baking dish from the Instant Pot and let the pizza cool. Slice in half.

Storing

Divide the pizza among 2 Ziploc bags and place in the freezer. Consume within 3 months. Thaw in the fridge overnight and heat in the microwave for a few minutes.

Nutrition facts per serving

Calories 390, Protein 8g, Total Carbs 30g, Fat 20g, Fiber 2g

Cinnamon Vanilla Oatmeal

Preparation time: 3 minutes | Cooking time: 10 minutes | Servings: 4

Ingredients

2 cups Steel Cut Oats
⅓ cup Brown Sugar
2 tsp Cinnamon Powder

1 ½ tsp Vanilla Extract
3 cups Water

Instructions

Place all the ingredients in your cooker. Stir well to combine. Seal the lid. You will know it is sealed once you hear the chime. Press "MANUAL" and set the cooking time to 10 minutes.

When you hear the beeping, release the pressure quickly. Open the lid and let the oatmeal cool completely.

Storing

When cooled, divide the oatmeal between 4 airtight containers. Enjoy for up to 4-6 days. To freeze, transfer to a container. Let set a little and put in the freezer.

Nutrition facts per serving

Calories 250, Protein 8g, Total Carbs 42g, Fat 3.5g, Fiber 9g

Hard-Boiled Eggs

Preparation time: 3 minutes | Cooking time: 7 minutes | Servings: 6

Ingredients

12 Eggs
1 cup of Water

Instructions

Pour the water into the Instant Pot and place the eggs inside. Put the lid on and turn it clockwise to close. You will know it is sealed once you hear the chime. Press "MANUAL" and cook on HIGH for 7 minutes.

When you hear the beeping, release the pressure quickly. Make sure to keep your hands away from the steam to avoid burning. Open the lid and remove the eggs from the water with tongs. Place in an ice bath and let cool completely.

Storing

When cooled, place the eggs in an airtight container and in the fridge. You can use them for up to 7-10 days. The egg whites are not freezer-friendly, but you can freeze the yolks for up to month or two.

Nutrition facts per serving

Calories 140, Protein 12g, Total Carbs 1.8g, Fat 9g, Fiber 0

Breakfast Ham Grits

Preparation time: 10 minutes | Cooking time: 5 minutes | Servings: 6

Ingredients

1 cup Quick-Cooking Grits

2 Shallots, diced

10 ounces Ham, chopped

1 cup grated Parmesan Cheese

3 tbsp Butter

2 cups Chicken Broth

Instructions

Set the Instant Pot to "SAUTE" and melt the butter. Add in shallots and ham, and cook for 4 minutes. Stir in the grits and broth and seal the lid. Select "MANUAL" and set the cooking time for 12 minutes on HIGH.

When you hear the beeping, release the pressure quickly b Open the lid and stir in the Parmesan Cheese. Set the Instant Pot to "SAUTE" and cook for a few more minutes with the lid off, until thickened. Allow to cool completely.

Storing

Divide between 6 airtight containers and put in the fridge for up to 3 days. To freeze, divide between 6 Ziploc bags or airtight containers and place in the freezer for up to 3 months.

Nutrition facts per serving

Calories 300, Protein 19g, Total Carbs 20g, Fat 13g, Fiber 6g

Chorizo Beans

Preparation time: 5 minutes | Cooking time: 40 minutes | Servings: 6

Ingredients

4 ounces Chorizo, chopped

3 cups Chicken Broth

1 tbsp Olive Oil

1 Onion, diced

2 tsp minced Garlic

2 cups dry Pinto Beans, soaked overnight

14 ounce canned diced Tomatoes

2 Bay Leaves

Instructions

Set your Instant Pot to "SAUTE" and add the oil. When hot and sizzling, add the chorizo and cook for about 3 minutes. When crispy, stir in the onions and garlic and cook until they are fragrant. Place all the other ingredients inside and stir well to combine.

Put the lid on and turn it clockwise to close. You will know it is sealed once you hear the chime. Press "MANUAL" and set the cooking time to 35 minutes. Cook on HIGH.

When you hear the beeping, press "KEEP WARM/CANCEL" to turn the Instant Pot off. Release the pressure naturally by letting the valve drop on its own. Open the lid and allow the beans to cool completely.

Storing

When cooled, divide between 4 airtight containers and place in the fridge. It's best to enjoy for 3 days. To freeze, divide between 6 Ziploc bags and arrange in a single layer in the freezer. When frozen, stack as desired. They will be good for up to 3 months.

Nutrition facts per serving

Calories 395, Protein 36g, Total Carbs 20g, Fat 18g, Fiber 6g

SNACKS AND SAIDE DISHES

Parmesan-Crusted Potato Fries

Preparation time: 10 minutes | Cooking time: 5 minutes | Servings: 4

Ingredients

4 Large Potatoes, peeled and sliced into strips
4 tbsp grated Parmesan Cheese
2 tbsp Butter, melted
1 tbsp Olive Oil
1 cup Water

Instructions

Pour the water into the Instant Pot and lower the rack. Arrange the potato strips on the rack and put the lid on. Seal by turning clockwise. You should hear a chime. When sealed, choose "MANUAL" and set the cooking time to 3 minutes. Cook on HIGH pressure.

When you hear the beeping, press "KEEP WARM/CANCEL" to turn the Instant Pot off. Release the pressure quickly by moving the pressure release handle from "Sealing" to "Venting". Open the lid and transfer potatoes to a plate.

Brush them with the butter and coat with parmesan cheese. Discard the water from the Instant Pot and wipe it clean. Select the "SAUTE" key and add the oil to it. When hot, add the potato fries and cook until golden. Let cool before storing.

Storing

When cooled, divide between 4 airtight containers. Place in the fridge for up to 3-4 days. To freeze, divide among 4 Ziploc bags and place in the freezer for up to 3 months.

Nutrition facts per serving

Calories 280, Protein 8g, Total Carbs 58g, Fat 2g, Fiber 8.8g

Sweet Beet Slices

Preparation time: 10 minutes | Cooking time: 20 minutes | Servings: 6

Ingredients

1 ½ pounds Baby Beets, peeled and sliced
½ Butter Stick
Pinch of Salt
1 cup Brown Sugar
1 cup Water

Instructions

Pour the water into the Instant Pot and lower the rack. Arrange the beet slices on the rack and close the lid. Seal by turning clockwise.

When sealed, choose "MANUAL" and set the cooking time to 15 minutes. Cook on HIGH pressure.

After the beep, press "KEEP WARM/CANCEL" to turn the Instant Pot off.

Release the pressure quickly by moving the handle to "Venting". Open the lid and transfer the beets to a bowl.

Discard the water and wipe the Instant Pot clean. Press the "SAUTE" key and add the butter to it. Stir in sugar and salt and cook for a minute.

Add the beets and cook until they are candied and well glazed, about 4 minutes. Let cool before storing.

Tip: If you want to turn the slices into chips, place on a lined baking sheet and bake at 350 degrees F in your oven for about 45 minutes.

Storing

When cooled, divide between 4 small Ziploc bags (avoid containers because they will become red in color). Place in the fridge. You can use them for up to 3 days. To freeze, divide among 4 Ziploc bags and place in the freezer for up to 3 months. Defrost in microwave and heat for a few minutes.

Nutrition facts per serving

Calories 240, Protein 2g, Total Carbs 43g, Fat 8g, Fiber 5g

Chili Kale Chips

Preparation time: 10 minutes | Cooking time: 4 minutes | Servings: 4

Ingredients

1 pound Kale, stems removed
1 tbsp Olive Oil
2 tsp Chili Powder
¼ tsp Garlic Powder
3 tbsp Lime Juice
½ cup Water

Instructions

Select the "SAUTE" key and add the oil to the Instant Pot. When sizzling, add the chili and garlic powder and cook for a couple of seconds before adding the washed kale leaves. Drizzle with the lime juice and close the lid.

Turn clockwise. When sealed, choose "MANUAL" and set the cooking time to 3 minutes. Cook on HIGH pressure.

When you hear the beeping, press "KEEP WARM/CANCEL" to turn the Instant Pot off. Release the pressure quickly by moving the pressure release handle from "Sealing" to "Venting". Open the lid and transfer to a plate. If you want it to be crispy, place under broiler for a few minutes.

Storing

When cooled, divide between 4 airtight containers and add other snacks alongside. Place in the fridge. You can enjoy the kale for up to a week. To freeze, divide among 4 Ziploc bags and place in the freezer for up to 3 months. Defrost in microwave and heat for a few minutes.

Nutrition facts per serving

Calories 66, Protein 2.3g, Total Carbs 8g, Fat 4g, Fiber 2.4g

Mixed Veggie Burgers

Preparation time: 10 minutes | Cooking time: 9 minutes | Servings: 4

Ingredients

1 bag Mixed Frozen Veggies
1 cup Flax Meal
2 tbsp Olive Oil
1 cup Cauliflower Florets
2 tbsp grated Parmesan Cheese
Salt and Pepper, to taste
1 ½ cups Water

Instructions

Pour the water into the Instant Pot. Place all the veggies in the steamer basket and lower into the pot. Put the lid on, turn clockwise to seal, and choose "MANUAL". Set the cooking time to 4 minutes. Cook on HIGH pressure.

After the beep, press the "CANCEL" button. Move the handle from "Sealing" to "Venting" to release the pressure quickly. When the pressure is fully released, open the lid. Transfer the veggies to a bowl and mash with a potato masher. Stir in the remaining ingredients, except the oil. Allow to cool. When safe to handle, shape the mixture into 4 burger patties.

Discard the cooking liquid from the Instant Pot and wipe it clean. Set to "SAUTE" and add the oil to it. Add the burger patties and cook for about 3 minutes per side, or until golden. Cool before storing.

Storing

Store in airtight containers in the fridge. Consume within 3 days. To freeze, divide among 4 Ziploc bags and place in the freezer. Consume within 3 months. Thaw in the fridge overnight and heat in the microwave for a few minutes.

Nutrition facts per serving

Calories 220, Protein 4g, Total Carbs 6g, Fat 10g, Fiber 3g

Turmeric Sweet Potato Sticks

Preparation time: 10 minutes | Cooking time: 3 minutes | Servings: 4

Ingredients

1 pound Sweet Potatoes, peeled and cut into sticks
½ tsp Garlic Powder
½ tsp Onion Powder
1 tsp Turmeric Powder
1 tbsp melted Butter
1 cup Water

Instructions

Place the potato sticks in a bowl and add the turmeric, onion, and garlic powder. Add butter and toss to coat well. Place in the steamer basket. Pour the water into the Instant Pot and lower the basket with the potato sticks into the Instant Pot. Put the lid on and seal it by turning clockwise. Select "MANUAL" and cook for 3 minutes on HIGH pressure.

When you hear the beeping, release the pressure quickly by moving the pressure release handle from "Sealing" to "Venting". Open the lid and remove the basket from the Instant Pot. Allow to cool.

Storing

When cooled, divide between 4 airtight containers. You can add some cream cheese, hummus, or other dip and veggies to the container. Place in the fridge for up to 3 days. To freeze, divide among 4 Ziploc bags and place in the freezer for up to 3 months.

Nutrition facts per serving

Calories 115, Protein 2g, Total Carbs 24g, Fat 1.5g, Fiber 3g

Scotch Eggs

Preparation time: 10 minutes | Cooking time: 9 minutes | Servings: 4

Ingredients:

4 Hard-boiled Eggs
1 cup Water
1 pound ground Chorizo Sausage
1 tbsp Olive Oil

Instructions

Roll out the chorizo and divide into 4 pieces. Wrap each egg in chorizo carefully. Select the "SAUTE" key and add the oil to the Instant Pot. When hot, add the Scotch eggs and cook until browned. Remove from the Instant Pot.

Pour the water into the Instant Pot and lower the rack. Place the eggs on the rack. Put the lid on and turn it clockwise. When sealed, choose "MANUAL" and set the cooking time to 6 minutes. Cook on HIGH pressure.

When you hear the beeping, release the pressure quickly by moving the pressure release handle from "Sealing" to "Venting". Open the lid and transfer to a plate.

Storing

When cooled, divide between airtight containers and place in the fridge. Consume within 2-3 days. To freeze, divide among 4 Ziploc bags and place in the freezer for up to 2-3 months. Defrost overnight in the fridge, and heat in the microwave.

Nutrition facts per serving

Calories 600, Protein 33g, Total Carbs 3g, Fat 50g, Fiber 0g

Parsley Cauliflower Tabbouleh

Preparation time: 10 minutes | Cooking time: 5 minutes | Servings: 6

Ingredients

1 cup chopped Parsley

2 cups Cauliflower Rice (ground in a food processor)

⅓ cup sliced Spring Onions

1 cup diced Tomatoes

1 tsp minced Garlic

3 tbsp Lemon Juice

1 tbsp chopped Mint

4 tbsp Olive Oil

Instructions

Select the "SAUTE" key and add 1 tbsp of oil to the Instant Pot. When hot, add the garlic and cook for about a minute. When fragrant, stir in the tomatoes and cauliflower. Sauté for 2-3 minutes. Stir in the remaining ingredients and transfer to a bowl.

Storing

When cooled, divide between 3 airtight containers. Place in the fridge and consume within 3-4 days. To freeze, divide among 3 Ziploc bags and place in the freezer. Consume within 3 months. Defrost in the microwave and heat for a couple of minutes to enjoy warm.

Nutrition facts per serving

Calories 110, Protein 1g, Total Carbs 2g, Fat 9g, Fiber 1.5g

Cabbage with Lemon and Coconut

Preparation time: 10 minutes | Cooking time: 10 minutes | Servings: 4

Ingredients

1 Cabbage, shredded

1 Onion, sliced

1 Carrot, sliced

1 tbsp Coconut Oil

½ cup desiccated Coconut

½ tsp Curry Powder

⅓ cup Fresh Lemon Juice

1 tsp minced Garlic

Instructions

Set the Instant Pot to "SAUTE" and add the coconut oil to it. When melted, add the onions and cook for 3 minutes, or until translucent.

Add garlic and cook for 30-60 seconds. Add the rest of the ingredients and give the mixture a good stir. Seal the lid and hit "MANUAL" after the chime and set the cooking time to 5 minutes. Cook on HIGH. Press "CANCEL" after the beep. Let the pressure drop naturally. When the float valve is down, open the lid. Allow to cool completely before storing.

Storing

When cooled, divide between 4 airtight containers. Place in the fridge; consume within 3 days. To freeze, place in the freezer. Consume within 3 months.

Nutrition facts per serving

Calories 190, Protein 4.5g, Total Carbs 20g, Fat 11g, Fiber 5g

Prosciutto-Dressed Asparagus

Preparation time: 10 minutes | Cooking time: 3 minutes | Servings: 4

Ingredients

8 Prosciutto Slices

1 pound Asparagus Spears, trimmed

1 cup Water

Instructions

Pour the water into the Instant Pot and lower the rack. Slice the prosciutto into strips so you can wrap every single asparagus spear in prosciutto. Arrange on the rack and put the lid on. Turn clockwise. When sealed, choose "MANUAL" and cook tfor 3 minutes on HIGH.

When you hear the beeping, release the pressure quickly. Open the lid and transfer the asparagus to a plate. Let cool before storing.

Storing

When cooled, divide between 4 airtight containers. Place in the fridge for up to 3 days. To freeze, divide among 4 Ziploc bags and place in the freezer for up to 3 months.

Nutrition facts per serving Calories 112, Protein 9g, Total Carbs 5.2g, Fat 6.5g, Fiber 2.4g

Sweet Toasted Walnuts

Preparation time: 10 minutes | Cooking time: 12 minutes | Servings: 4

Ingredients

2 cups Walnut Halves
⅓ cup Honey or Maple Syrup
½ tsp Cinnamon
½ cup plus 1 tbsp Water

Instructions

In a bowl, place the honey, walnuts, 1 tbsp water, and cinnamon. Stir well to coat and dump the mixture into the Instant Pot.

Select the "SAUTE" button and cook for 5 minutes with the lid off. Line a baking dish with some parchment paper and transfer the walnuts to it.

Pour the water into the Instant Pot and lower the rack. Place the baking dish on the rack and put the lid on. When sealed, choose "MANUAL" and cook for 12 minutes on HIGH pressure. After the timer goes off, release the pressure quickly by switching the pressure release handle from "Sealing" to "Venting". Allow to cool completely.

Storing

When cooled, store in airtight containers in the fridge for up to a week. To freeze, store in Ziploc bags. Let the pecans thaw in the fridge before consuming.

Nutrition facts per serving

Calories 460, Protein 5g, Total Carbs 31g, Fat 39g, Fiber 25g

'Fried' Cinnamon Banana

Preparation time: 5 minutes | Cooking time: 5 minutes | Servings: 4

Ingredients

½ cup Coconut Oil
4 Bananas, sliced
¼ tsp Cinnamon

Instructions

Set the pot to "SAUTE" and place coconut oil inside; cook until melted. Add in the cinnamon and cook for a few seconds. Stir in banana slices. Cook for 2 minutes and then flip over and cook for 2 more. Transfer the bananas to a bowl and let cool before storing.

Storing

When cooled, divide between 4 airtight containers. Place in the fridge for up to 2 days.

Nutrition facts per serving

Calories 280, Protein 1.3g, Total Carbs 27g, Fat 20g, Fiber 3g

Lemony Potato Dip

Preparation time: 10 minutes | Cooking time: 10 minutes | Servings: 4

Ingredients

2 Sweet Potatoes

¼ cup Lemon Juice

¼ tsp Lemon Zest

¼ tsp Lemon Pepper

2 tbsp Sour Cream

¼ tsp Garlic Powder

¼ tsp Onion Powder

1 tbsp Olive Oil

Instructions

Pour the water in the Instant Pot and lower the rack. Peel the potatoes and cut in half lengthwise. Place on the rack and close the lid. Turn clockwise. When sealed, choose "MANUAL" and set the cooking time to 10 minutes. Cook on HIGH pressure.

When you hear the beeping, release the pressure quickly. Open the lid and transfer the potatoes to a bowl. Add the remaining ingredients and mash until smooth.

Storing

Divide between 4 airtight containers and add some veggies to the containers for dipping, as well baby carrots, celery sticks, etc. Place in the fridge. You can use them for up to 3 days.

Nutrition facts per serving

Calories 145, Protein 1.5g, Total Carbs 12g, Fat 10g, Fiber 1.7g

Red Potatoes with Herbs

Preparation time: 10 minutes | Cooking time: 6 minutes | Servings: 4

Ingredients

2 pounds Red Potatoes, quartered

1 ½ cup Water

2 tbsp chopped Cilantro

2 tbsp chopped Parsley

6 tbsp Butter or Coconut Oil, melted

6 Garlic Cloves, minced

2 tbsp chopped Basil

Instructions

Pour the water into the baking dish and lower the rack. Combine all the ingredients in a baking dish that can fit in the Instant Pot. Place the baking dish on the rack and close the lid of the Instant Pot. To seal, turn clockwise. When you hear the chime, hit "MANUAL" and set the cooking time to 6 minutes. Cook on HIGH.

Press "CANCEL" after the beep. Do a quick pressure release by moving the pressure handle from "Sealing" to "Venting". Open the lid and remove the baking dish from the Instant Pot.

Storing

When cooled, divide between 4 airtight containers. Place in the fridge and consume within 3-4 days. To freeze, divide among 4 Ziploc bags and place in the freezer for up 3 months.

Nutrition facts per serving

Calories 320, Protein 6g, Total Carbs 43g, Fat 15g, Fiber 4g

Sweet and Sticky Party Chicken Wings

Preparation time: 10 minutes | Cooking time: 10 minutes | Servings: 6

Ingredients

20 Chicken Wings
2 cups Water
3 tbsp Tamari Sauce
3 tbsp Tomato Paste
3 tbsp Honey
1 tbsp Olive Oil
1 tbsp Brown Sugar
¼ tsp Liquid Smoke, optional
¼ tsp Onion Powder
¼ tsp Garlic Powder

Instructions

Pour the water into the Instant Pot and place the chicken wings inside. Put the lid on and turn it clockwise. After the chime, choose "MANUAL" and set the cooking time to 5 minutes. Cook on HIGH pressure.

When you hear the beeping, release the pressure quickly by turning the handle to "Venting". Open the lid and transfer the wings to a bowl.

Whisk all the remaining ingredients and brush over the chicken wings. Discard the cooking water from the Instant Pot and wipe it clean. Place the chicken wings inside and set it to "SAUTE". Cook for a few minutes, or until sticky. Let cool before storing.

Storing

When cooled, divide between 4 airtight containers. Place in the fridge for up to 3 days. To freeze, divide among 4 Ziploc bags and place in the freezer for up to 3 months.

Nutrition facts per serving

Calories 220, Protein 21g, Total Carbs 19g, Fat 6g, Fiber 1g

Baba Ghanoush

Preparation time: 10 minutes | Cooking time: 9 minutes | Servings: 4

Ingredients

2 Eggplants, peeled and sliced
1 tbsp minced Garlic
1 ½ tbsp Sesame Paste
¼ cup chopped Parsley
2 tbsp Olive Oil
1 tsp Salt
2 tsp Canola Oil
¾ cup Water

Instructions

Set the Instant Pot to "SAUTE" and add the canola oil to it. Add the eggplants and cook for 3 minutes. Stir in the garlic and cook for another minute. Pour the water over.

Put the lid on and turn it clockwise to seal. Select "MANUAL" and set the cooking time to 5 minutes. Cook on HIGH pressure.

When you hear the beeping, release the pressure quickly. Open the lid and transfer the mixture to a food processor. Add the remaining ingredients and pulse until smooth. Let cool completely before storing.

Storing

When cooled, divide between 4 airtight containers. Add veggies for dipping in the containers. Place in the fridge. You can use them for up to 4-6 days. To freeze, divide among 4 Ziploc bags and place in the freezer for up to 3 months. Defrost in the fridge overnight.

Nutrition facts per serving

Calories 200, Protein 5g, Total Carbs 21g, Fat 11g, Fiber 4g

Mediterranean Dip

Preparation time: 10 minutes | Cooking time: 10 minutes | Servings: 6

Ingredients

28 ounces canned diced Tomatoes
½ cup sliced Black Olives
4 tbsp grated Parmesan Cheese
½ cup Basil Leaves
4 Garlic Cloves, crushed
1 cup chopped Carrots
½ Onion, chopped
¾ cup Chicken Broth
1 tbsp Olive Oil
Salt and Pepper, to taste

Instructions

Choose the "SAUTE" key and turn on the Instant Pot. Add the oil to it and heat until sizzling. Add onions and garlic and cook for 2-3 minutes. Stir in the tomatoes, carrots, basil, and broth. Lock the lid and choose "MANUAL". With the help of '+' and '-' buttons, set the cooking time to 8 minutes. Cook on HIGH pressure.

When you hear the beeping, press "KEEP WARM/CANCEL" to turn the Instant Pot off. Release the pressure quickly by turning the handle to "Venting". Open the lid and transfer to a food processor. Stir in the remaining ingredients and pulse until smooth.

Let cool completely before storing.

Storing

When cooled, divide between 4 airtight containers. Add some veggies (carrot sticks, celery sticks, cucumber strips, etc.) for dipping. Place in the fridge. Consume for up to 3 days. To freeze, divide among 4 Ziploc bags and place in the freezer for up to 3 months. Defrost in the fridge.

Nutrition facts per serving

Calories 120, Protein 4g, Total Carbs 15g, Fat 5g, Fiber 5g

Crab Bites

Preparation time: 10 minutes | Cooking time: 4 minutes | Servings: 4

Ingredients

1 cup Crab Meat
1 tbsp Olive Oil
1 Carrot, shredded
¼ cup sliced Black Olives
¼ cup Almond Flour
¼ cup Chicken Stock
2 tbsp diced Onion
4 tbsp Parmesan Cheese
½ cup mashed Potatoes

Instructions

Place the carrots, potatoes, crab meat, olives, flour, and onion in a bowl. Mix with your hand until the mixture is well combined. Make balls out of the mixture and roll them in parmesan cheese.

Set the Instant Pot to "SAUTE" and add the oil to it. When hot, add the crab bites and cook until they are golden on all sides. Transfer to a plate and let cool before storing.

Storing

When cooled, divide between 4 airtight containers. Place in the fridge. You can use them for up to 3 days. To freeze, divide among 4 Ziploc bags and place in the freezer for up to 3 months. Defrost in the fridge overnight and heat in the microwave for a minute or so.

Nutrition facts per serving

Calories 130, Protein 9g, Total Carbs 3g, Fat 4g, Fiber 1g

Tuna Melt

Preparation time: 10 minutes | Cooking time: 10 minutes | Servings: 4

Ingredients

2 Tuna Cans, drained
½ cup Breadcrumbs
½ cup shredded Cheddar Cheese
1 Egg
¼ cup Flour

Instructions

You don't need water for this recipe as you will not be bringing it to pressure.

In a bowl, combine the tuna, half of the breadcrumbs, and shredded cheese. Make balls out of the mixture and set aside. In another bowl, beat the egg.

Select "SAUTE" and grease the Instant Pot with some cooking spray. Dip the tuna balls in flour first, then in egg, and finally, coat them with breadcrumbs. Place in the Instant Pot and cook until they become golden and crispy on all sides. Transfer to a plate and let cool completely.

Storing

When cooled, divide between 4 airtight containers. Place in the fridge for up to 3 days. To freeze, divide among 4 Ziploc bags and place in the freezer for up to 3 months.

Nutrition facts per serving

Calories 220, Protein 23g, Total Carbs 16g, Fat 7g, Fiber 1g

Maple and Cinnamon Carrot Sticks

Preparation time: 10 minutes | Cooking time: 8 minutes | Servings: 4

Ingredients

1 ½ cup Carrot Sticks
¼ cup Maple Syrup
½ tsp Cinnamon
2 tbsp Butter
1 cup Water

Instructions

Pour the water into the Instant Pot and lower the rack. Arrange the carrot sticks on the rack and put the lid on. To seal, turn it clockwise. Choose "MANUAL" and set the cooking time to 3 minutes. Cook on HIGH pressure.

When you hear the beeping, do a quick pressure release. Transfer the carrots to a plate.

Discard the water and wipe the Instant Pot clean. Select the "SAUTE" key and add the butter. When melted, stir in the maple and cinnamon. Add the carrot sticks and stir to coat well. Cook for a few minutes, or until glazed. Let cool completely before storing.

Storing

When cooled, divide between 4 airtight containers. Place in the fridge for up to 4-6 days. To freeze, divide among 4 Ziploc bags and place in the freezer for up to 3 months.

Nutrition facts per serving

Calories 172, Protein 0.5g, Total Carbs 31g, Fat 6g, Fiber 1.3g

Salmon Veggie Noodles

Preparation time: 10 minutes | Cooking time: 5 minutes | Servings: 4

Ingredients

4 Salmon Filets
1 Bell Pepper, spiralized
1 Zucchini, spiralized
2 Carrots, spiralized
A handful of parsley, chopped
1 tbsp Olive Oil
1 Rosemary Sprig
1 cup Water
Juice of ½ Lemon

Instructions

Pour the water into the Instant Pot and place the rosemary sprig inside. In a bowl, place the veggie noodles, parsley, and lemon juice. Toss to combine. Lower the rack in the Instant Pot and place the veggies on it. Top with the salmon filets. Drizzle the oil over and put the lid on. Close and turn clockwise. When sealed, choose "MANUAL" and set the cooking time to 5 minutes. Cook on HIGH pressure.

When you hear the beeping, release the pressure quickly. Open the lid and allow to cool.

Storing

When cooled, divide the veggies between 4 airtight containers and top with salmon. Place in the fridge for up to 3 days. To freeze, divide among 4 Ziploc bags and place in the freezer for up to 3 months. Defrost in microwave and heat for a few minutes.

Nutrition facts per serving

Calories 310, Protein 40g, Total Carbs 9g, Fat 13g, Fiber 3g

Maple Squash Cubes

Preparation time: 10 minutes | Cooking time: 10 minutes | Servings: 6

Ingredients

½ cup Butter, melted
1 pound Butternut Squash, peeled and cut into cubes
1 cup Water
¼ cup Maple Syrup

Instructions

Pour the water into the Instant Pot and place the squash cubes inside. Put the lid on and turn it clockwise. After the chime, choose "MANUAL" and set the cooking time to 7 minutes. Cook on HIGH pressure.

When you hear the beeping, release the pressure quickly. Transfer the squash to a bowl.

Discard the cooking liquid and wipe the Instant Pot clean. Set it to "SAUTE" and place the butter inside. When melted, stir in the maple syrup. Add the squash cubes and give it a good stir until well coated. Cook for a few minutes, until glazed. Let cool before storing.

Storing

When cooled, divide between 6 airtight containers. Place in the fridge. You can use them for up to 3-4 days. To freeze, divide among 6 small Ziploc bags and place in the freezer for up to 3 months. Defrost in microwave and heat for a few minutes

Nutrition facts per serving

Calories 245, Protein 2g, Total Carbs 20g, Fat 16g, Fiber 3g

Curried Jacket Potatoes

Preparation time: 5 minutes | Cooking time: 20 minutes | Servings: 4

Ingredients

1 ½ pounds Sweet Potatoes
1 tbsp melted Butter
1 tsp Curry Powder
1 cup Water

Instructions

Pour the water into the Instant Pot and lower the rack. Wash the potatoes well and prick the skin with a fork. Place them on the lowered rack. Drizzle with melted butter and sprinkle with curry powder. Close the lid and turn it clockwise to seal. After the chime, choose "MANUAL" and set the cooking time to 20 minutes. Cook on HIGH pressure.

When you hear the beeping, release the pressure quickly. Open the lid and transfer the potatoes to a plate. Let cool completely. Slice into quarters.

Storing

When cooled, divide between 4 airtight containers and add some cheese and dips alongside. Place in the fridge. You can use them for up to 3 days. To freeze, divide among 4 Ziploc bags and place in the freezer for up to 3 months.

Nutrition facts per serving

Calories 170, Protein 2g, Total Carbs 31g, Fat 4g, Fiber 4g

Chili Cheesy Corn Bowl

Preparation time: 10 minutes | Cooking time: 2 minutes | Servings: 4

Ingredients

2 cups canned Corn
½ cup crumbled Feta Cheese
1 tbsp chopped Cilantro
1 Garlic Clove, minced
2 tsp Chili Powder
¼ tsp Smoked Paprika
Juice of ½ Lime

Instructions

Heat the olive oil in the Instant Pot on "SAUTE". When sizzling, add the spices and garlic and cook for one minute. Add the corn and cook for an additional minute, until well coated and fragrant. Add the remaining ingredients and give the mixture a good stir. Transfer to a bowl. Let cool completely before storing.

Storing

When cooled, divide between 4 airtight containers. Place in the fridge. You can use them for up to 3 days. To freeze, divide among 4 small Ziploc bags and place in the freezer for up to 3 months. Defrost in microwave and heat for a few minutes.

Nutrition facts per serving

Calories 120, Protein 6g, Total Carbs 14.5g, Fat 4.5g, Fiber 2.4g

Peanut Chicken Noodles

Preparation time: 5 minutes | Cooking time: 10 minutes | Servings: 6

Ingredients

1 ½ pounds Chicken Breasts, cut into cubes

1 cup Peanut Sauce

5 ounces Rice Noodles

1 cup Sugar Snap Peas

¾ cup Chicken Broth

Instructions

Combine the chicken and peanut sauce in the Instant Pot. Close the lid and turn it clockwise to seal. When you hear the chime, set to "MANUAL". With the "+" and "-" buttons, set the cooking time to 8 minutes. Cook on HIGH.

After the beep, release the pressure quickly. Stir in the noodles and broth. Close the lid again and cook for 2 more minutes. Do a quick pressure release. Let the noodles cool completely.

Storing

When cooled, transfer to 6 airtight containers and place in the fridge for up to 3 days. To freeze, divide among 6 Ziploc bags and place in the freezer for up to 3 months.

Nutrition facts per serving

Calories 670, Protein 63g, Total Carbs 83g, Fat 26g, Fiber 16g

Mint and Lime Zoodles

Preparation time: 10 minutes | Cooking time: 4 minutes | Servings: 4

Ingredients

½ tsp Lime Zest

¼ cup Lime Juice

4 Zucchini, spiralized

1 tsp minced Garlic

¼ cup chopped Mint

2 tbsp Olive Oil

1 tbsp Butter

Instructions

Click on "SAUTE" and add the oil to the Instant Pot. When hot, add the lime zest and garlic and cook for 30-60 seconds. Add all the remaining ingredients. Give the mixture a good stir and cook for about 2-3 minutes. Let cool completely before storing.

Storing

When cooled, divide between 4 airtight containers. Place in the fridge and consume within 4-6 days. To freeze, divide among 4 Ziploc bags and place in the freezer. Consume within 3-6 months. Defrost in the fridge overnight and heat for a few minutes.

Nutrition facts per serving

Calories 180, Protein 4g, Total Carbs 12g, Fat 15g, Fiber 1g

Farro, Bean, and Mushroom Bake

Preparation time: 10 minutes | Cooking time: 20 minutes | Servings: 4

Ingredients

1 tsp minced Garlic

1 ½ cups Navy Beans

2 ½ cups sliced Mushrooms

¾ cup Farro

4 Green Onions, chopped

3 tbsp minced Shallots

1 tbsp diced Jalapenos

1 cup diced Tomatoes

Instructions

Place all the ingredients in the Instant Pot. Stir to combine and put the lid on. Turn clockwise to seal. Hit "MANUAL" after the chime and set the cooking time to 20 minutes. Cook on HIGH pressure.

Press "CANCEL" after the beep. Let the pressure out quickly by moving the handle to "Venting". Open the lid and let the mixture cool completely before storing.

Storing

When cooled, divide between 4 airtight containers. Place in the fridge and consume within 3 days. To freeze, divide among 4 Ziploc bags and place in the freezer. Consume within 3 months.

Defrost in the fridge overnight or in the microwave and heat for a few minutes.

Nutrition facts per serving

Calories 250, Protein 5g, Total Carbs 17g, Fat 2g, Fiber 5g

Chili Carrot Mash

Preparation time: 15 minutes | Cooking time: 4 minutes | Servings: 4

Ingredients

1 ½ pounds Carrots, chopped
1 ½ cups Water
1 tbsp Butter
1 tbsp Coconut Cream
1 tsp Chili Powder

Instructions

Pour the water into the Instant Pot. Place the carrots in the steamer basket and the lower the basket into the pot. Close the lid and turn clockwise to seal.

After the chime, select the "MANUAL" cooking mode. Set the cooking time to 4 minutes and cook on HIGH pressure.

When the timer goes off, move the handle to "Venting" to release the pressure quickly. When the pressure is fully released, open the lid. Transfer the veggies to a food processor. Add the remaining ingredients and pulse until smooth. Let cool before storing.

Storing

Divide the mashed carrots between 4 airtight containers. Place in the fridge and consume within 3 days. To freeze, transfer in freezer molds or ice cube tray. Consume within 1-2 months.

Nutrition facts per serving

Calories 45, Protein 1g, Total Carbs 11g, Fat 1g, Fiber 1g

Parmesan Risotto

Preparation time: 10 minutes | Cooking time: 15 minutes | Servings: 4

Ingredients

2 ½ cups Chicken Broth

2 Onions, diced

½ cup grated Parmesan Cheese

1 ½ cups Rice

1 ½ cups Sparkling Wine

½ tsp Thyme

1 tsp minced Garlic

2 tbsp Butter

Instructions

Set the Instant Pot to "SAUTE" and add the butter to it. When melted, add the onions and sauté for 3 minutes. Add garlic and cook for one more minute. Stir in the rice and cook for an additional minute. Add broth and wine, stir to combine and close the lid. Turn it clockwise to seal. You should hear a chime. Select "MANUAL" and cook on HIGH for 10 minutes.

When the timer goes off, move the handle to "Venting" to release the pressure quickly. Stir in the thyme and parmesan cheese and allow to cool completely before storing.

Storing

Divide the risotto between 4 airtight containers. Place in the fridge and consume within 3 days. To freeze, divide among 4 Ziploc bags and place in the freezer. Consume within 3 months. Defrost in the fridge overnight or in the microwave and heat to enjoy warm.

Nutrition facts per serving

Calories 490, Protein 18g, Total Carbs 64g, Fat 13g, Fiber 8g

Spaghetti Bolognese

Preparation time: 5 minutes | Cooking time: 10 minutes | Servings: 4

Ingredients

1 pound ground Beef
1 tbsp Olive Oil
1 tsp minced Garlic
½ Onion, diced
24 ounces Marinara Sauce
½ pound Spaghetti
¼ tsp Basil
¼ tsp Oregano

Instructions

Heat the oil in the Instant Pot on "SAUTE". Add the onions and cook for about 3 minutes. Add the garlic and cook for one more. When fragrant, add the beef and cook for a few minutes, or until it becomes browned. Add the remaining ingredients to the pot.

Put the lid on and turn it clockwise to close. You will know it is sealed once you hear the chime. Press "MANUAL" and cook on HIGH for 5 minutes. After the Instant Pot beeps, release the pressure quickly. Open the lid and allow the pasta to cool completely.

Storing

Divide between 4 airtight containers and place in the fridge for up to 3-4 days. To freeze, divide between Ziploc bags and place in a single layer in your freezer. When frozen, store as you like. Enjoy for up to 3 months.

Nutrition facts per serving

Calories 440, Protein 42g, Total Carbs 55g, Fat 17g, Fiber 8g

Ham and Chicken White Penne

Preparation time: 10 minutes | Cooking time: 15 minutes | Servings: 4

Ingredients

1 cup Broth
2 Chicken Breasts, diced
¼ cup Breadcrumbs
¼ cup crushed Crackers
½ pound cooked Ham, diced
1 tbsp Butter
1 ½ cups shredded Cheese
½ pound Penne
½ cup Heavy Cream

Instructions

Place the chicken, broth, ham, and pasta in your Instant Pot. Give it a good stir to combine and put the lid on. Turn it clockwise to seal. After the chime, set the Instant Pot to "MANUAL" and cook on HIGH for 7 minutes.

When you hear the beeping, release the pressure quickly. Open the lid and stir in the remaining ingredients. Set your Instant Pot to "SAUTE" and cook for about 5 minutes with the lid off. Allow the pasta to cool completely.

Storing

When cooled, divide the pasta between 4 airtight containers and place in the fridge. You can enjoy for up to 3 days. To freeze, divide between 4 Ziploc bags and arrange in the freezer in a single layer. You can stack the bags on top once they are frozen. Enjoy for 2 months. Defrost in the microwave and microwave for a few minutes before serving.

Nutrition facts per serving

Calories 580, Protein 46g, Total Carbs 42g, Fat 38g, Fiber 5g

Stewed Fennel Chickpeas

Preparation time: 10 minutes | Cooking time: 20 minutes | Servings: 4

Ingredients

2 cups Chickpeas

3 tsp minced Garlic

1 Fennel Bulb, chopped

½ cup chopped Scallions

½ cup grated Parmesan Cheese

1 tbsp Olive Oil

4 cups Veggie Broth

Salt and Pepper, to taste

Instructions

Set your Instant Pot to "SAUTE" and add the oil to it. When hot and sizzling, add the fennel, scallions, and garlic. Cook for a minute or so. Add chickpeas and broth, stir to combine.

Put the lid on. Turn it clockwise to seal. After the chime, select the "MANUAL" cooking mode, and set the cooking time to 20 minutes. Cook on HIGH.

When the timer goes off, press the "CANCEL" button. Move the handle to "Venting" to release the pressure quickly. When the pressure is fully released, open the lid.

Drain the excess liquid and transfer the chickpeas to a bowl. Stir in the parmesan cheese and let cool completely.

Storing

Divide between 4 airtight containers. Place in the fridge and consume within 3 days. To freeze, divide among 4 Ziploc bags and place in the freezer. Consume within 3 months.

Nutrition facts per serving

Calories 374, Protein 20g, Total Carbs 50g, Fat 11g, Fiber 12g

Kale Cauliflower Rice

Preparation time: 10 minutes | Cooking time: 10 minutes | Servings: 4

Ingredients

½ Onion, diced
6 cups ground Cauliflower
1 cup Veggie Broth
¼ cup Coconut Milk
2 cups chopped Kale
1 tsp minced Garlic
¼ cup grated Parmesan Cheese

Instructions

Select "SAUTE" and place the oil in the Instant Pot. When hot and sizzling, add the onions and sauté for 3-4 minutes. When soft, add the garlic and cook for one more minute.

Add the remaining ingredients, except the cheese, and stir well to combine. Put the lid on and turn it clockwise to seal. You should hear the chime. Choose "MANUAL" and set the cooking time to 5 minutes. Cook on HIGH.

After the beep, press the "CANCEL" button. Move the handle from "Sealing" to "Venting" to release the pressure quickly. When the pressure is fully released, open the lid. Stir in the parmesan and let cool completely.

Storing

Divide the rice between 4 airtight containers. Place in the fridge and consume within 3 days. To freeze, divide among 4 Ziploc bags and place in the freezer. Consume within 3 months. Thaw in the fridge overnight or defrost in the microwave and heat in the microwave for a few minutes.

Nutrition facts per serving

Calories 120, Protein 3g, Total Carbs 7g, Fat 5g, Fiber 2g

Baby Root Veggie Bake

Preparation time: 10 minutes | Cooking time: 16 minutes | Servings: 6

Ingredients

½ cup Veggie Broth
1 Onion, diced
2 pounds Baby Carrots
4 pounds Baby Potatoes, halved
2 tbsp Olive Oil
1 Garlic Clove, minced

Instructions

Select "SAUTE" and place the oil in the Instant Pot. When hot and sizzling, add the onions and sauté them for 3 minutes. When translucent, add the garlic and cook for one more minute. Add the carrots and potatoes and pour the broth over. Put the lid on and turn it clockwise to seal. After the chime, select the "MANUAL" cooking mode, and set the cooking time to 10 minutes. Cook on HIGH.

When the timer goes off, move the handle to "Venting" to release the pressure quickly. When the pressure is fully released, open the lid. Allow the veggies to cool.

Storing

Divide the veggies between 4 airtight containers. Place in the fridge and consume within 3-4 days. To freeze, divide among 4 Ziploc bags and place in the freezer for up 3 months.

Nutrition facts per serving

Calories 330, Protein 7g, Total Carbs 65g, Fat 5g, Fiber 8g

Instant Broccoli and Mushrooms

Preparation time: 5 minutes | Cooking time: 8 minutes | Servings: 4 as a side dish

Ingredients

1 cup sliced Mushrooms

1 cup Veggie Broth

2 tbsp Butter or Coconut Oil

2 cups Broccoli Florets

¼ tsp Paprika

1 tbsp Tamari

¼ tsp Garlic Powder

Instructions

Set the Instant Pot to "SAUTE". Melt the butter, add the mushrooms and cook for 4-5 minutes. Stir in the broccoli and tamari and cook for additional minute. Pour in the broth and seal the lid. Select the "MANUAL" key and set the cooking time to 2 minutes.

When the timer goes off, release the pressure quickly. When the pressure is fully released, open the lid. Drain the veggies and transfer to a bowl. Let cool completely.

Storing

Divide the veggies between 2 airtight containers. Place in the fridge and consume within 3-4 days. To freeze, divide among 2 Ziploc bags and place in the freezer for up 3 months.

Nutrition facts per serving

Calories 80, Protein 2g, Total Carbs 4g, Fat 2g, Fiber 1g

Creamy Mushroom Pasta

Preparation time: 10 minutes | Cooking time: 9 minutes | Servings: 4

Ingredients

1 ½ cups sliced Mushrooms

2 cups Water

2 cups Pasta

1 cup Heavy Cream

¼ cup grated Parmesan Cheese

1 tsp Cornstarch

1 tbsp Butter

Instructions

Select "SAUTE" and place the butter in the Instant Pot. When melted, add the mushrooms and cook for 4 minutes. Add the remaining ingredients, except the cheese and sela the lid.

Turn clockwise to seal. Select the "MANUAL" cooking mode after the chime and set the cooking time to 7 minutes. Cook on HIGH.

When the timer goes off, press the "CANCEL" button. Move the handle to "Venting" to release the pressure quickly. When the pressure is fully released, open the lid. Stir in the parmesan immediately. Wait to cool before storing.

Storing

Divide the pasta between 4 airtight containers. Place in the fridge and consume within 3 days. To freeze, divide among 4 Ziploc bags and place in the freezer. Consume within 3 months. Thaw in the fridge overnight and heat in the microwave for a few minutes.

Nutrition facts per serving

Calories 450, Protein 15g, Total Carbs 34g, Fat 15g, Fiber 3g

Pesto Farfalle

Preparation time: 10 minutes | Cooking time: 8 minutes | Servings: 4

Ingredients

4 cups Water

¾ cup Pesto Sauce

12 ounces Farfalle

1 cup Cherry Tomatoes, halved

Instructions

In the Instant Pot, combine the water and farfalle. Put the lid on and seal by turning clockwise. Select the "MANUAL" key and set the cooking time to 7 minutes with the help of the '+' and '-' buttons. Cook on HIGH.

When the timer goes off, press the "CANCEL" button. Move the handle from "Sealing" to "Venting" for a quick pressure release. When the pressure is fully released, open the lid. Stir in the pesto immediately. Fold in the tomatoes.

Storing

Divide the pasta between 4 airtight containers. Place in the fridge and consume within 3 days. To freeze, divide among 4 Ziploc bags and place in the freezer. Consume within 3 months. Thaw in the fridge overnight and heat in the microwave for a few minutes.

Nutrition facts per serving

Calories 390, Protein 8g, Total Carbs 40g, Fat 9g, Fiber 1g

Lemony and Garlicky Steamed Asparagus

Preparation time: 8 minutes | Cooking time: 2 minutes | Servings: 4

Ingredients

16 ounces Asparagus Spears, trimmed

3 tbsp Lemon Juice

1 tbsp Olive Oil

2 tsp minced Garlic

¼ tsp Garlic Powder

¼ tsp Lemon Zest

1 ½ cups Water

Instructions

Pour the water into the Instant Pot. Lace the asparagus spears in the steamer basket and lower it into the pot. Whisk together the remaining ingredients in a bowl and drizzle this mixture over the asparagus. Put the lid on and seal by turning clockwise. Select "STEAM" and set the cooking time to 2 minutes.

When the timer goes off, press the "CANCEL" button. Move the handle to "Venting" to release the pressure quickly. When the pressure is fully released, open the lid. Remove the asparagus from the pot and let cool.

Storing

Store in airtight containers. Place in the fridge and consume within 3 days. To freeze, divide among Ziploc bags and place in the freezer. Consume within 3 months. Defrost in the microwave and heat in the microwave for a few minutes.

Nutrition facts per serving

Calories 95, Protein 2.7g, Total Carbs 4.5g, Fat 7g, Fiber 2g

Red Bean Patties

Preparation time: 5 minutes | Cooking time: 20 minutes | Servings: 4

Ingredients

2 cups mashed Potatoes

2 cups Red Beans

¼ cup Breadcrumbs

2 cups Water

1 ½ tbsp Olive Oil

Salt and Pepper, to taste

Instructions

Combine the water and beans in the Instant Pot. Put the lid on, turn clockwise to seal, and choose the "MANUAL" cooking mode. Set the cooking time to 15 minutes. Cook on HIGH.

When the timer goes off, press the "CANCEL" button. Move the handle to "Venting" to release the pressure quickly. When the pressure is fully released, open the lid. Drain the beans and transfer to a bowl. Add the potatoes and breadcrumbs and season with salt and pepper. Mix with your hands and shape 4 patties out of the mixture.

Discard the water from the Instant Pot and wipe the Instant Pot clean. Set it to "SAUTE" and add the oil. When hot, add the patties and cook for a few minutes, or until golden on both sides. Let cool before storing.

Storing

Store in the fridge in airtight containers. Best if consumed within 3 days. To freeze, divide among 4 Ziploc bags and place in the freezer. Consume within 3 months. Thaw in the fridge overnight and heat in the microwave for a few minutes.

Nutrition facts per serving

Calories 250, Protein 10g, Total Carbs 48g, Fat 2g, Fiber 10g

Cheesy Asparagus Pasta

Preparation time: 5 minutes | Cooking time: 9 minutes | Servings: 4

Ingredients

1 cup shredded Cheese

3 ½ cups Veggie Broth

2 cups Pasta

½ cup Alfredo Sauce

6 Asparagus Spears, chopped

Instructions

Combine the broth and pasta in the Instant Pot. Close the lid, turn clockwise to seal, and hit "MANUAL". Set the cooking time to 7 minutes and cook on HIGH pressure.

When you hear the beep, release the pressure quickly. Drain the pasta and discard the cooking liquid. Set the Instant Pot to "SAUTE" and return the pasta to the inner pot. Stir in the sauce and cheese and cook for 2 minutes. Let cool before storing.

Storing

Divide the pasta between 4 airtight containers. Place in the fridge and consume within 3 days. To freeze, divide among 4 Ziploc bags and place in the freezer. Consume within 3 months. Thaw in the fridge overnight and heat in the microwave for a few minutes.

Nutrition facts per serving

Calories 480, Protein 8g, Total Carbs 39g, Fat 12g, Fiber 2g

POULTRY AND SEAFOOD

Spinach Coconut Chicken

Preparation time: 10 minutes | Cooking time: 15 minutes | Servings: 4

Ingredients

1 ⅓ pounds Chicken Breasts, cubed
1 cup chopped Spinach
⅔ cup Chicken Broth
⅓ cup Coconut Cream
5 tbsp chopped Basil
1 tsp minced Garlic
1 tbsp Olive Oil
Salt and Pepper, to taste

Instructions

Select the "SAUTE" key and add the olive oil to the Instant Pot. When hot, add the garlic and cook for a minute. Add the chicken and make sure to cook it until it becomes brown on all sides. Add the remaining ingredients and stir well to combine. Put the lid on and turn it clockwise. Select "MANUAL" and set the cooking time to 8 minutes on HIGH pressure.

After the beep, release the pressure quickly. Open the lid and let sit until completely cooled.

Storing

When cooled, divide between 4 airtight containers. Place in the fridge. You can use them for up to 3 days. To freeze, divide among 4 Ziploc bags and place in the freezer for up to 3 months. Defrost the chicken in your microwave and heat for a few minutes to enjoy warm.

Nutrition facts per serving

Calories 320, Protein 35g, Total Carbs 4g, Fat 14g, Fiber 1g

Lemongrass Drumsticks

Preparation time: 15 minutes | Cooking time: 18 minutes | Servings: 4

Ingredients

8 Chicken Drumsticks

1 Lemongrass Stalk, trimmed and smashed

2 whole Garlic Cloves, smashed

1 tsp grated Ginger

1 Onion, sliced

1 tsp Five Spice Powder

2 tbsp Tamari

1 tbsp Butter

1 cup Coconut Milk

Instructions

Place the coconut milk, lemongrass, ginger, garlic, tamari, and spice powder in a blender. Blend until the mixture becomes smooth. Set aside.

Select "SAUTE" and melt the butter in the Instant Pot. Cook the onions until they are soft, about 3 minutes. Place the drumsticks inside and pour in the coconut mixture. Put the lid on and turn it clockwise. Select "MANUAL" and cook for 15 minutes. Cook on HIGH pressure.

When the screen reads 0:00, turn the Instant Pot off by pressing "CANCEL". Release the pressure quickly by moving the pressure handle from "Sealing" to "Venting". Open the lid when the pressure is fully released.

Storing

When cooled, divide between 4 airtight containers. Make sure to divide the sauce as well. Place in the fridge. Use for up to 3 days. To freeze, divide among 4 Ziploc bags and place in the freezer for up to 3 months. Defrost in the fridge overnight and heat for a few minutes in the microwave.

Nutrition facts per serving

Calories 216, Protein 27g, Total Carbs 9.5g, Fat 7g, Fiber 1g

Gingery Turkey Meatballs

Preparation time: 10 minutes | Cooking time: 15 minutes | Servings: 4

Ingredients

1 pound ground Turkey
1 tbsp Olive Oil
2 tsp Sesame Oil
½ cup Coconut Aminos
3 tbsp Coconut Flour
1 ½ tsp grated Ginger

Instructions

Combine the turkey and coconut flour in a bowl. Mix with your hands until the mixture is fully incorporated. Shape into 24 meatballs.

Select "SAUTE" and add the olive oil to the Instant Pot. Add the meatballs and cook them until they become golden on all sides. Meanwhile, whisk the remaining ingredients together in a bowl. Pour the mixture over the meatballs and close the lid. After the chime, select "MANUAL" and set the cooking time to 10 minutes on HIGH.

After the beep, turn the Instant Pot off by pressing "KEEP WARM / CANCEL". Release the pressure naturally by letting the float valve drop on its own. Open the lid and let the meatballs cool completely.

Storing

When cooled, take 4 airtight containers and place 6 meatballs in each of them. Place in the fridge. Consume within 3 days. To freeze, divide among 4 Ziploc bags and place in the freezer for up to 3 months. Defrost in the microwave or in the fridge overnight and heat for a few minutes in order to consume warm.

Nutrition facts per serving

Calories 250, Protein 23g, Total Carbs 5.5g, Fat 17g, Fiber 1g

Tomato and Kale Turkey

Preparation time: 10 minutes | Cooking time: 14 minutes | Servings: 4

Ingredients

1 ½ pounds Turkey Breasts, chopped

1 tbsp Olive Oil

1 cup chopped Kale

1 cup canned diced Tomatoes

½ cup Coconut Milk

⅔ cup Chicken Stock

¼ tsp Onion Powder

¼ tsp Paprika

Instructions

Set your Instant Pot to "SAUTE". Add the oil and heat until sizzling. Add the spices and turkey and cook for a few minutes, until the turkey is cooked through and no longer pink. Pour the stock over and close the lid. Press "MANUAL" and set the cooking time to 4 minutes on HIGH pressure.

When the timer goes off, release the pressure quickly. Stir in the rest of the ingredients. Close the lid and cook for 4 minutes on HIGH. Release the pressure quickly again. Let the turkey cool completely before storing.

Storing

When cooled, divide between 4 airtight containers. Place in the fridge. Consume within 3 days. To freeze, divide among 4 Ziploc bags and place in the freezer in a single layer. When frozen, stack as desired. The turkey will be safe to consume for up to 3 months.

Nutrition facts per serving

Calories 455, Protein 55g, Total Carbs 3g, Fat 26g, Fiber 1g

Sweet Potato Chicken Curry

Preparation time: 10 minutes | Cooking time: 22 minutes | Servings: 4

Ingredients

16 ounces Chicken Breasts, cut into cubes

2 cups Green Beans, trimmed

2 tsp Butter

1 Onion, diced

1 Sweet Potato, cubed

2 ounces Heavy Cream or Coconut Milk

½ cup Broth

2 tbsp Curry Powder

1 tsp Turmeric Powder

1 tsp minced Garlic

Instructions

Set your Instant Pot to "SAUTE" and place the butter inside. When melted, add the onions and cook for 3 minutes. When translucent, add the garlic and cook for 1 more minute. Add the chicken and cook until it becomes golden. Pour the broth over and put the lid on. Turn it clockwise to close. You will know it is sealed once you hear the chime. Press "MANUAL" and cook on HIGH for 10 minutes.

When you hear the beeping, press "KEEP WARM/CANCEL" to turn the Instant Pot off. Release the pressure quickly by moving the pressure release handle from "Sealing" to "Venting". Make sure to keep your hands away from the steam to avoid burning. Open the lid and stir in the remaining ingredients. Seal the lid again and cook for another 3 minutes on HIGH. Again, release the pressure quickly. Open the lid and allow for the curry to cool completely.

Storing

When cooled, divide between airtight containers and store in the fridge. It will be delicious for up to 3-4 days. To freeze, transfer to a container and place in the freezer. When set and not so runny, divide between 4 Ziploc bags and arrange in a single layer. When frozen, store as you desire. Enjoy for up to 4 months.

Nutrition facts per serving

Calories 290, Protein 28g, Total Carbs 21g, Fat 10g, Fiber 4g

Mushroom and Leek Turkey Casserole

Preparation time: 10 minutes | Cooking time: 17 minutes | Servings: 6

Ingredients

1 ¼ pounds Mushrooms, sliced

2 pounds Turkey Breasts, chopped

4 tbsp Butter

2 Leeks, sliced

½ cup Milk

2 tbsp Arrowroot

¼ tsp Garlic Powder

Salt and Pepper, to taste

Instructions

Set the Instant Pot to "SAUTE" and add the butter to it. When melted, add the turkey cubes and cook them for a few minutes, until they are no longer pink. Transfer to a plate. Add the leeks and mushrooms to the Instant Pot and cook for 3 minutes. Return the turkey to the Instant Pot along with the broth and garlic powder. Stir to combine and close the lid. Turn it clockwise to seal. After the chime, select "MANUAL" and set the cooking time to 8 minutes on HIGH.

Turn the Instant Pot off by pressing "CANCEL" after the beep. Release the pressure quickly by turning the handle from "Sealing" to "Venting". Open the lid when the pressure is fully released. Whisk together the milk and arrowroot and stir the mixture into the Instant Pot. Set to "SAUTE" and cook for 2 minutes or until thickened. Let cool completely before storing.

Storing

When cooled, divide between 4 airtight containers. Place in the fridge and consume within 3 days. Simply heat in the microwave. To freeze, divide among 4 Ziploc bags and place in the freezer in a single layer. When frozen, you can stack the bags on top of each other. Freeze for up to 3 months. Defrost in the fridge overnight and heat for a few minutes.

Nutrition facts per serving

Calories 555, Protein 50g, Total Carbs 37g, Fat 22g, Fiber 3g

Chicken, Bean, and Tomato Bake

Preparation time: 5 minutes | Cooking time: 15 minutes | Servings: 6

Ingredients

1 pound Chicken Breasts, diced
1 pound canned stewed Tomatoes
1 tbsp Olive Oil
1 pound canned Kidney Beans
2 cups Chicken Stock
⅓ cup Sour Cream
½ tsp Paprika
Salt and Pepper, to taste

Instructions

Dump all the ingredients in the Instant Pot and add some salt and pepper to it. Stir to combine everything well and close the lid. Turn it clockwise to seal. When you hear a chime, select "POULTRY" and set the cooking time to 15 minutes on HIGH.

Turn the Instant Pot off by pressing "CANCEL" after the beep. Release the pressure quickly by turning the handle from "Sealing" to "Venting".

Storing

When cooled, divide between 4 airtight containers. Place in the fridge and consume within 2-3 days. To freeze, divide among 4 Ziploc bags and place in the freezer in a single layer for up to 2-3 months. Defrost in the fridge overnight and heat for a few minutes.

Nutrition facts per serving

Calories 350, Protein 5g, Total Carbs 22g, Fat 8g, Fiber 6g

Enchilada Chicken Casserole with Cauliflower

Preparation time: 10 minutes | Cooking time: 15 minutes | Servings: 6

Ingredients

1 cup shredded Cheddar Cheese

½ cup Salsa Verde

2 cups cooked and shredded Chicken

20 ounces Cauliflower Florets, chopped

4 ounces Cream Cheese

¼ cup Sour Cream

Salt and Pepper, to taste

1 ½ cups Water

Instructions

Pour the water into the Instant Pot and lower the trivet. Grease a baking dish with cooking spray and combine all the ingredients in it. Season with salt and pepper. Place the baking dish on the trivet and put the lid on. Turn clockwise and set the Instant Pot to "MANUAL" after the sealing chime sounds. Set the cooking time to 15 minutes and cook on HIGH.

When you hear the beeping, release the pressure quickly. Open the lid and remove the baking dish from the Instant Pot. Let cool completely.

Storing

When cooled, divide among 6 airtight containers and place in the fridge for up to 3 days. To freeze, divide among 6 Ziploc bags and place in the freezer for up to 3 months.

Nutrition facts per serving

Calories 311, Protein 33g, Total Carbs 5.2g, Fat 18g, Fiber 1.2g

Garlicky Shredded Chicken

Preparation time: 10 minutes | Cooking time: 20 minutes | Servings: 4

Ingredients

1 ¾ pounds Chicken Breasts

1 ½ tsp Garlic Powder

1 cup Chicken Broth

¼ tsp Black Pepper

Instructions

Place all the ingredients in the Instant Pot. Put the lid on and turn it clockwise. Select "MANUAL" and cook for 20 minutes on HIGH pressure.

After the beep, release the pressure quickly Grab two forks and shred the meat inside the pot. Stir to combine with the liquid well. Let cool completely before storing.

Storing

When cooled, divide between 4 airtight containers. Place in the fridge for up to 3 days.

Nutrition facts per serving

Calories 420, Protein 41g, Total Carbs 1g, Fat 17g, Fiber 0g

Mexican-Spiced Chicken

Preparation time: 10 minutes | Cooking time: 50 minutes | Servings: 4

Ingredients

1 ½ pounds Chicken Breasts
1 Jalapeno, deseeded and diced
28 oz canned Tomatoes with Green Chilies

½ Cumin
¼ tsp Cayenne Pepper
½ tsp Paprika

Instructions

Place all the ingredients in the Instant Pot. Give the mixture a good stir and put the lid on. Seal by turning clockwise. Select "MANUAL" and set the cooking time to 25 minutes with the '+' and '-' buttons. Cook on HIGH pressure.

After the beep, release the pressure quickly. Grab two forks and shred the chicken inside the pot immediately. Stir to combine. Allow to cool before storing.

Storing

When cooled, divide between 4 airtight containers or Ziploc bags in the fridge for up to 3 days. To freeze, divide among 4 Ziploc bags and place in the freezer for up to 3 months.

Nutrition facts per serving

Calories 320, Protein 38g, Total Carbs 13g, Fat 10g, Fiber 4g

Sweet Cumin and Ginger Chicken

Preparation time: 10 minutes | Cooking time: 25 minutes | Servings: 4

Ingredients

4 Chicken Breasts, diced
1 tbsp Cornstarch
1 cup Chicken Stock
1 cup Coconut Sugar
1 ½ tsp Cumin Powder
2 tsp grated Ginger
2 tbsp Olive Oil

Instructions

Set the Instant Pot to "SAUTE" and heat oil until sizzling. Toss the chicken with the cornstarch. Place the chicken inside the Instant Pot and cook until it becomes golden. Add the ginger and cumin and cook for 30 more seconds. Stir in all the remaining ingredients and seal the lid. Select "MANUAL" and set the cooking time to 20 minutes on HIGH.

Turn the Instant Pot off by pressing "CANCEL" after the beep. Allow the pressure to come down naturally. When the float valve is down and the pressure is fully released, open the lid.

Storing

When cooled, divide between 4 airtight containers. Place in the fridge and consume within 3 days. To freeze, transfer to 4 Ziploc bags and place in the freezer for up to 3 months.

Nutrition facts per serving

Calories 640, Protein 55g, Total Carbs 46g, Fat 27g, Fiber 0g

Green Olives and Onion Chicken

Preparation time: 10 minutes | Cooking time: 18 minutes | Servings: 4

Ingredients

1 pound Chicken Breasts
2 tbsp Lemon Juice
1 Red Onion, sliced
1 can pitted Green Olives
2 tbsp Butter
1 cup Chicken Stock

Instructions

Select "SAUTE" and turn on your Instant Pot. Melt the butter and cook the onions for 3 minutes. When they become translucent, add the chicken. Cook for a few minutes, or until golden on all sides. Stir in the rest of the ingredients. Close the lid and turn it clockwise to seal. Select "MANUAL" and set the cooking time to 10 minutes. Cook on HIGH pressure.

After the beep, release the pressure quickly. Let cool completely before storing.

Storing

When cooled, divide the chicken along with the olives and onion between 4 airtight containers. Place in the fridge and consume within 3 days.

Nutrition facts per serving

Calories 500, Protein 44g, Total Carbs 2g, Fat 34g, Fiber 1g

Stewed Mussels and Scallops Lunch

Preparation time: 5 minutes | Cooking time: 12 minutes | Servings: 4

Ingredients

1 Onion, diced
2 Bell Peppers, diced
1 cup Scallops
2 cups Mussels
1 cup Rice
2 ¼ cups Chicken Stock
1 tbsp Olive Oil

Instructions

Heat the oil in your Instant Pot on "SAUTE" and add the peppers and onions. Cook for a few minutes, or until soft. Add the rice and cook for one more minute. Stir in the scallops and cook for another minute. Place the rest of the ingredients inside and stir well to combine.

Put the lid on and seal it by turning it clockwise. After you hear the chime, select "MANUAL" and set the cooking time for 6 minutes. Cook on HIGH.

When you hear the beeping, press "KEEP WARM/CANCEL" to turn the Instant Pot off. Release the pressure quickly naturally by allowing the valve to drop on its own. Open the lid and let cool completely.

Storing

Divide between 4 airtight containers and put in the fridge. You can use them for up to 3 days. To freeze, divide between 4 Ziploc bags or airtight containers and place in the freezer for up to 3 months. Defrost in the fridge and microwave for a few minutes before serving.

Nutrition facts per serving

Calories 200, Protein 20g, Total Carbs 13g, Fat 5g, Fiber 3.7g

Cheesy Prawn Casserole

Preparation time: 10 minutes | Cooking time: 15 minutes | Servings: 4

Ingredients

1 ½ pound Prawns

2 cans diced Tomatoes

2 tbsp chopped Parsley

½ Onion, diced

1 cup shredded Cheese

¼ cup Breadcrumbs

½ cup Broth

2 tbsp Butter

Instructions

Set the Instant Pot to "SAUTE" and melt the butter. Add the onions and cook for 3 minutes until translucent; stir in tomatoes, broth, and parsley. Put the lid on, turn clockwise and set to "MANUAL". Set the cooking time to 9 minutes and cook on HIGH.

When you hear the beeping, release the pressure quickly. Stir in the shrimp. Close the lid again and cook for 2 minutes. Do a quick pressure release and stir in the breadcrumbs and cheddar. Cook for an additional minute with the lid off on "SAUTE".

Storing

Divide the salad among 4 airtight containers and place in the fridge for up to 3 days. To freeze, divide among 4 Ziploc bags and place in the freezer for up to 3 months.

Nutrition facts per serving

Calories 330, Protein 22g, Total Carbs 13.5g, Fat 16g, Fiber 2.5g

BEEF AND PORK

Beef Barbacoa

Preparation time: 10 minutes | Cooking time: 65 minutes | Servings: 8

Ingredients

2 pounds Chuck Roast
1 tbsp Cumin
1 Onion, sliced
½ cup Water
8 ounces Green Chilies, diced
Juice of 2 Limes
2 tsp minced Garlic
1 tsp Oregano

Instructions

Place all the ingredients, except the beef, in a bowl. Stir to combine. Place the beef in the Instant Pot and pour the sauce over. Seal the lid and click on the "MANUAL" button and let the beef cook for 1 hour.

Release the pressure quickly by turning the handle from "Sealing" to "Venting". Grab two forks and shred the meat inside the pot. Stir to combine, set the Instant Pot to "SAUTE", and cook for another 2 minutes, or until slightly thickened. Let cool completely before storing.

Storing

When cooled, divide between 8 airtight containers. Place in the fridge and consume within 3 days. To freeze, divide among 8 Ziploc bags and freeze. Consume within 3 months. Defrost in the fridge overnight and heat for a few minutes.

Nutrition facts per serving

Calories 355, Protein 33g, Total Carbs 34g, Fat 22g, Fiber 1g

Dijon Meatloaf

Preparation time: 15 minutes | Cooking time: 35 minutes | Servings: 4

Ingredients

1 Egg
1 pound Ground Beef
½ cup Almond Flour
2 tbsp Dijon Mustard
½ tsp Thyme
1 cup Water
½ tsp Garlic Powder
1 Onion, diced
¼ cup Tomato Sauce

Instructions

Pour the water into the Instant Pot and lower the trivet. Ina bowl, add all the remaining ingredients. Mix with your hand to combine well. Grease a baking dish or a loaf pan with some cooking spray. Press the meatloaf mixture into it. Place the dish on top of the trivet and close the lid. Turn it clockwise to seal. After the chime, select "MANUAL" and set the cooking time to 35 minutes on HIGH.

Turn the Instant Pot off by pressing "CANCEL" after the beep. Release the pressure quickly by turning the handle from "Sealing" to "Venting". Open the lid and remove the baking dish from the Instant Pot. Allow to cool completely. Slice into thin slices.

Storing

Divide the meatloaf slices between 4 airtight containers. Place in the fridge and consume within 3 days. Simply heat in the microwave. To freeze, divide among 4 Ziploc bags and place in the freezer. Consume within 3 months. Defrost in the fridge overnight and heat for a few minutes.

Nutrition facts per serving

Calories 410, Protein 41g, Total Carbs 38g, Fat 10g, Fiber 3g

Beef Cubes with Zucchini and Tomatoes

Preparation time: 10 minutes plus 3 hours | Cooking time: 25 minutes | Servings: 4

Ingredients

1 pound Beef, cubed

½ Onion, diced

1 Zucchini, diced

1 tbsp Butter

2 Large Tomatoes, diced

1 tsp minced Garlic

1 tsp minced Ginger

½ cup Heavy Cream

Instructions

In a bowl, combine the beef, heavy cream, garlic, and ginger. Cover the bowl and place in the fridge. Let the beef marinate for 3 hours. Place the beef and the marinade in the Instant Pot, along with everything except the zucchini. Close the lid and turn it clockwise. When sealed, select "MANUAL" and set the cooking time for 20 minutes.

Turn the Instant Pot off by pressing "CANCEL" after the beep. Move the handle to "Venting" and allow the pressure to come out quickly. Open the lid and stir in the zucchini. Set the Instant Pot to "SAUTE" and cook until the zucchini becomes tender, about 4-5 minutes.

Let cool completely before storing.

Storing

When cooled, divide between 4 airtight containers (or one large if you are planning on serving it all at once). Place in the fridge and consume within 3 days. To freeze, divide among 4 Ziploc bags and place in the freezer. Freeze for up to 3 months. Defrost in the fridge overnight and heat for a few minutes.

Nutrition facts per serving

Calories 340, Protein 24g, Total Carbs 13g, Fat 22g, Fiber 3g

Beef Ribs and White Button Mushrooms

Preparation time: 10 | Cooking time: 25 minutes | Servings: 4

Ingredients

2 pounds Beef Ribs

2 ½ cups Bone Broth

1 cup sliced Carrots

2 cups quartered Button Mushrooms

1 Onion, chopped

¼ cup Tomato Sauce

¼ tsp Cumin

2 tbsp Olive Oil

¼ tsp Pepper

Instructions

Set your Instant Pot to "SAUTE" and add the oil to it. When hot, add the ribs and cook them on all sides until browned. Add all the remaining ingredients to the Instant Pot and stir well to combine. Close the lid and turn it clockwise.Select "MANUAL" cook for 20 minutes.

Turn the Instant Pot off by pressing "CANCEL" after the beep. Move the pressure handle from "Sealing" to "Venting" to release the pressure quickly.

Storing

When cooled, divide between 4 airtight containers (the ribs on one side and the mushroom mixture on the other side of the container). Place in the fridge and consume within 3 days. To freeze, divide among 4 Ziploc bags and place in the freezer. Freeze for up to 3 months. Defrost in the fridge overnight and heat for a few minutes.

Nutrition facts per serving

Calories 525, Protein 50g, Total Carbs 8g, Fat 29g, Fiber 3g

Gorgonzola Beef Medley with Cabbage

Preparation time: 10 minutes | Cooking time: 45 minutes | Servings: 6

Ingredients

1 pound Steak, cut into slices

6 ounces Gorgonzola Cheese, crumbled

1 Onion, diced

1 cup chopped Parsnips

1 cup sliced Carrots

1 quart Bone Broth

2 cups canned diced Tomatoes

½ Cabbage, diced

Salt and Pepper, to taste

Instructions

Set the Instant Pot to "SAUTE" and grease with some cooking spray. Add the beef and sear on all sides, until browned. Dump everything else, except the cheese, in the Instant Pot, stir to combine, and put the lid on. Seal by turning it clockwise. After you hear the chime, select "MANUAL" and set the cooking time for 40 minutes. Cook on HIGH.

When you hear the beeping, press "KEEP WARM/CANCEL" to turn the Instant Pot off. Release the pressure quickly by moving the pressure release handle from "Sealing" to "Venting". Make sure to keep your hands away from the steam to avoid burning. Open the lid and stir in the gorgonzola immediately. Allow the medley to cool completely.

Storing

Divide the medley between 6 airtight containers and put in the fridge. You can use them for up to 3 days. To freeze, divide between 6 Ziploc bags or airtight containers and place in the freezer for up to 3 months. Defrost in the fridge and microwave for a couple of minutes to enjoy warm.

Nutrition facts per serving

Calories 420, Protein 8.5g, Total Carbs 52g, Fat 23g, Fiber 7g

Chili Con Carne

Preparation time: 10 minutes | Cooking time: 15 minutes | Servings: 6

Ingredients

28 ounces canned diced Tomatoes
14 ounces canned Kidney Beans, drained
14 ounces canned Black Beans, drained
1 ½ pounds Ground Beef
1 tsp Cumin
1 tbsp Worcestershire Sauce
½ cup Bell Peppers, chopped
1 Jalapeno, deseeded and diced
1 tbsp minced Garlic
2 tbsp Olive Oil
1 tbsp Chili Powder
1 Onion, diced
½ cup Water

Instructions

Set the Instant Pot to "SAUTE" and add the olive oil. When sizzling, add the onions and garlic and cook until fragrant. Add the beef and cook until it becomes browned. Add the bell peppers and cook for 2 more minutes. Stir in the spices and cook for an additional minute. Add the rest of the ingredients and give it a good stir. Close the lid and turn clockwise so you seal it properly. Select "MANUAL" and set the cooking time to 10 minutes on HIGH.

When you hear the beeping, release the pressure quickly. Allow the chili to cool completely.

Storing

When cooled, transfer the chili to 6 airtight containers and place in the fridge for up to 3 days. To freeze, divide among 6 Ziploc bags and place in the freezer for up to 3 months. Defrost in microwave and heat for a few minutes.

Nutrition facts per serving

Calories 690, Protein 53g, Total Carbs 73g, Fat 24g, Fiber 15g

Paleo Stuffed Peppers

Preparation time: 10 minutes | Cooking time: 25 minutes | Servings: 4

Ingredients

½ Onion, diced
4 Bell Peppers
1 Tomato, diced
1 pound ground Beef
5 tbsp Coconut Flour
1 cup Tomato Sauce
1 Egg, beaten
⅔ cup Water
1 tsp Oregano

Instructions

In a bowl, combine the onion, beef, flour, tomatoes, oregano, and egg. Slice off the pepper tops and discard the seeds. Fill with the beef filling. In the Instant Pot, add the water and half of the tomato sauce and stir to combine. Place the stuffed peppers inside. Pour the remaining tomato sauce over the peppers. Put the lid on and turn clockwise to seal. Select "MANUAL" and set the cooking time to 15 minutes. Cook on HIGH pressure.

After the beep, let the float valve drop on its own for a natural pressure release. Open the lid and let the peppers cool completely.

Storing

When cooled, store in 4 airtight containers and place in the fridge. You can use them for up to 3 days. To freeze, divide among 4 Ziploc bags or containers and place in the freezer for up to 3 months. Defrost in microwave and heat for a few minutes.

Nutrition facts per serving

Calories 440, Protein 23g, Total Carbs 14g, Fat 32g, Fiber 5g

Lentils and Beef

Preparation time: 10 minutes | Cooking time: 30 minutes | Servings: 4

Ingredients

1 ½ cups Lentils, rinsed
½ pound Beef, cubed
1 cup chopped Scallions
5 cups Chicken Stock
1 tsp minced Garlic
1 cup sliced Carrots
1 cup chopped Celery
1 tbsp Oil

Instructions

Set the Instant Pot to "SAUTE" and heat the oil. When sizzling, add the garlic and cook for 1 minute. Add beef and cook until it becomes browned. Stir in the remaining ingredients. Put the lid on and turn it clockwise to close.

After the chime, hit "MANUAL" and cook on HIGH for 20 minutes. When you hear the beeping, release the pressure quickly. Open the lid and allow the lentils to cool completely.

Storing

When cooled, divide between 4 airtight containers and place in the fridge for 3 days. Or you can divide between Ziploc bags and place in the freezer for up to 3 months.

Nutrition facts per serving

Calories 372, Protein 26g, Total Carbs 51g, Fat 17g, Fiber 12g

Tomato Beef Brisket

Preparation time: 10 minutes | Cooking time: 50 minutes | Servings: 8

Ingredients

3 pounds Beef Brisket

2 tsp minced Garlic

28 ounces diced Tomatoes

1 cup Beef Stock

2 tbsp Olive Oil

1 Onion, chopped

Instructions

Set the Instant Pot to "SAUTE" and heat half the oil. Add the beef and sear on all sides until brown. Transfer to a plate. Heat the rest of the oil and place the onions and garlic inside. Cook for 2-3 minutes. Stir in the remaining ingredients and return the beef to the pot.

Close the lid and turn it clockwise. Select "MANUAL". Cook for 50 minutes on HIGH.

Turn the Instant Pot off by pressing "CANCEL" after the beep. Let the pressure drop on its own. When the valve is down, open the lid. Either shred with 2 forks or slice thinly.

Storing

When cooled, divide between 8 airtight containers in the fridge and consume within 3 days.

Nutrition facts per serving

Calories 410, Protein 50g, Total Carbs 8g, Fat 15g, Fiber 1.5g

Pork Shoulder with Orange and Cinnamon

Preparation time: 15 | Cooking time: 45 minutes | Servings: 10

Ingredients

5 pounds Pork Shoulder
2 Cinnamon Sticks
1 tbsp Cumin
2 cups fresh Orange Juice
2 tbsp Olive Oil
2 tsp minced Garlic
1 Jalapeno Pepper, diced
2 Bay Leaves
¼ tsp Garlic Powder
¼ tsp Thyme
¼ tsp Black Pepper

Instructions

In a small bowl, combine half of the oil with the spices. Rub the mixture into the meat. Set the Instant Pot to "SAUTE" and add the remaining oil to it.

When hot, add the pork and sear on all sides well. Transfer to a plate. Pour the orange juice into the Instant Pot and deglaze the bottom.

Add the remaining ingredients and return the pork to the pot. Close and seal the lid. Select "MANUAL" and set the cooking time for 40 minutes. Cook on HIGH

Turn the Instant Pot off by pressing "CANCEL" after the beep. Let the pressure drop on its own. When the float valve comes down, open the lid. Grab two forks and shred the meat within the pot. Stir to coat well and let cool completely.

Storing

When cooled, divide between 5 airtight containers (two servings per a container). Place in the fridge and consume within 3 days. To freeze, divide among 5 Ziploc bags (two servings per a bag) and place in the freezer. Freeze for up to 3 months.

Nutrition facts per serving

Calories 600, Protein 55g, Total Carbs 14g, Fat 55g, Fiber 3g

Sage Pork with Yams

Preparation time: 10 minutes | Cooking time: 38 minutes | Servings: 6

Ingredients

2 pounds Pork, cubed

2 Yams, peeled and cubed

2 tsp Sage

3 tbsp Tomato Paste

1 Bell Pepper, chopped

1 Onion, diced

2 tsp minced Garlic

1 tbsp Olive Oil

1 ½ cups Bone Broth

Instructions

Select the "SAUTE" button and preheat your Instant Pot. Add the oil to it. When hot, add the onions and cook for 3 minutes.

Once the onion becomes translucent, add the garlic and cook for one more minute. Stir in the pork and cook until it becomes browned on all sides.

Add the remaining ingredients and give the mixture a good stir. Put the lid on and turn clockwise to seal.

When you hear the chime, select the "MANUAL" cooking mode and set the time to 30 minutes. Cook on HIGH.

Turn the Instant Pot off by pressing "CANCEL" after the beep. Do a quick pressure release by moving the handle to "Venting". Open the lid and let the meat cool down completely before storing.

Storing

When cooled, divide between 6 airtight containers. Place in the fridge and consume within 3 days. To freeze, divide among 6 Ziploc bags and place in the freezer. Consume within 3 months. Defrost in the fridge overnight and heat for a few minutes.

Nutrition facts per serving

Calories 390, Protein 43g, Total Carbs 2g, Fat 28g, Fiber 1g

Bean & Pork Stew

Preparation time: 10 minutes | Cooking time: 30 minutes | Servings: 8

Ingredients

2 cups Pinto Beans, soaked overnight

1 pound Pork, cubed

2 Onions, diced

4 ½ cups Chicken Stock

1 tsp Paprika

1 Bay Leaf

1 tbsp Olive Oil

1 Garlic Clove, minced

Instructions

Press the "SAUTE" key and add the oil to the Instant Pot. When hot, add the onions and cook for 3 minutes. When they become translucent, add the garlic. Cook for 1 minute and add the pork. Make sure to brown it well on all sides. Stir in the remaining ingredients and put the lid on. Seal by turning clockwise and press "MEAT/STEW". Set the cooking time to 20 minutes.

When you hear the beeping, press "KEEP WARM/CANCEL" to turn the Instant Pot off. Release the pressure naturally by allowing the valve to come down on its own. When dropped, open the lid. Allow the stew to cool completely before storing.

Storing

When cooled, divide between 8 airtight containers and place in the fridge. You can use them for up to 3 days. To freeze, place in a container and in the freezer. When set, divide between 8 Ziploc bags and place in the freezer in a single layer. When completely frozen, stack as desired. The stew can be kept for up to 3 months.

Nutrition facts per serving

Calories 280, Protein 26g, Total Carbs 33g, Fat 8g, Fiber 7g

Chipotle Pork

Preparation time: 10 minutes | Cooking time: 55 minutes | Servings: 4

Ingredients

1 ½ pounds Pork Shoulder
½ tsp Paprika
2 Chipotle Peppers, diced
1 Onion, sliced
¼ tsp Pepper
½ tsp Cumin
½ tsp Garlic Powder
1 cup Beef Broth

Instructions

In a small bowl, combine all the spices. Rub the mixture into the pork. Place the pork in the Instant Pot and top with pepper and onion slices.

Pour the broth over and close the lid. Turn clockwise to seal. After the chime, select "MEAT/STEW" and set the cooking time for 55 minutes.

Turn the Instant Pot off by pressing "CANCEL" after the beep. Let the pressure come down on its own. Grab two forks and shred the meat within the Instant Pot. Let cool before storing.

Storing

When cooled, divide between 4 airtight containers. Place in the fridge for up 3 days. To freeze, divide among 4 Ziploc bags and place in the freezer. Consume within 3 months.

Nutrition facts per serving

Calories 510, Protein 49g, Total Carbs 2g, Fat 37g, Fiber 1g

Chili Braised Pork Chops

Preparation time: 10 | Cooking time: 23 minutes | Servings: 4

Ingredients

4 Pork Chops
1 tbsp Olive Oil
1 Onion, diced
2 tbsp Chili Powder
½ cup Beef Broth
14 ounces canned diced Tomatoes

Instructions

Set your Instant Pot to "SAUTE". Add the oil to it. When hot, add the onions and cook for 3 minutes. Stir in the chili and add the pork chops. Cook until they are browned on both sides. Add in tomatoes and broth. Seal the lid, select "MANUAL" and cook for 15 minutes.

Press "CANCEL" after the beep. Move the handle to "Venting" for a quick pressure release. Open the lid and allow to cool completely before storing.

Storing

When cooled, divide between 4 airtight containers. Place in the fridge and consume within 3 days. To freeze, divide among 4 Ziploc bags and place in the freezerfor up 3 months.

Nutrition facts per serving

Calories 440, Protein 45g, Total Carbs 1g, Fat 23g, Fiber 0.5g

Simple Buttery Pork Chops

Preparation time: 10 minutes | Cooking time: 17 minutes | Servings: 6

Ingredients

1 tbsp Steak Rub Seasoning
6 Pork Chops
8 tbsp Butter
1 tbsp Oil
1 cup Bone Broth

Instructions

Select the "SAUTE" key and heat the oil. Brown the pork chops well on all sides. Sprinkle with the seasoning and top with the butter. Pour in the broth and seal the lid. Select "MANUAL" cook for 12 minutes on HIGH. Turn the Instant Pot off by pressing "CANCEL" after the beep. Move the handle to "Venting" and allow the pressure to come out quickly.

Storing

When cooled, place the pork chops in airtight containers in the fridge for up to 3 days.

Nutrition facts per serving

Calories 430, Protein 22g, Total Carbs 0g, Fat 38g, Fiber 0g

DESSERT RECIPES

Banana Almond Butter Healthy Bars

Preparation time: 10 minutes | Cooking time: 15 minutes | Servings: 4

Ingredients

1 cup Almond Butter
6 Bananas, sliced
2 tbsp Cocoa Powder
1 ½ cups Water

Instructions

Pour the water into the Instant Pot and lower the rack. Grease a baking dish with cooking spray and set aside.

In a bowl, mash the bananas together with the almond butter. Stir in the cocoa powder and pour the mixture into the baking dish. Lace the baking dish on the rack and put the lid on. Turn clockwise. Choose "MANUAL" and set the cooking time to 15 minutes on HIGH.

When you hear the beeping, release the pressure quickly. Open the lid and remove the baking dish from the Instant Pot. Let cool completely and cut into bars.

Storing

Divide the bars between 4 airtight containers. Place in the fridge. You can use them for up to 3 days. To freeze, place in the freezer for up to 3 months. Defrost in the fridge overnight and warm to room temperature if you don't want them cold. Do not microwave!

Nutrition facts per serving

Calories 142, Protein 3g, Total Carbs 14g, Fat 10g, Fiber 2g

Apple Coconut Bowl

Preparation time: 10 minutes | Cooking time: 5 minutes | Servings: 4

Ingredients

2 Apples, peeled and diced
1 cup Coconut Milk
¼ cup Almond Flour
¼ cup shredded Coconut
Pinch of Cinnamon

Instructions

Add all the ingredients to Instant Pot. Stir to combine everything well and put the lid on. Turn it clockwise to seal properly. When sealed, choose "MANUAL" and set the cooking time to 5 minutes. Cook on HIGH pressure.

After the beep, press "KEEP WARM/CANCEL" to turn the Instant Pot off. Release the pressure quickly by moving the pressure release handle from "Sealing" to "Venting". Open the lid and transfer to a bowl. Let cool completely.

Storing

When cooled, divide between 4 small glass jars. Place in the fridge. You can use them for up to 2 days. To freeze, divide among 4 Ziploc bags and place in the freezer for up to 3 months. Defrost in microwave and heat for a few minutes.

Nutrition facts per serving

Calories 140, Protein 2g, Total Carbs 17g, Fat 8g, Fiber 3.5g

Almond and Coconut Cake

Preparation time: 15 minutes | Cooking time: 40 minutes | Servings: 8

Ingredients

½ cup Heavy Cream
1 cup Almond Flour
⅓ cup Honey
¼ cup Butter, melted
2 Eggs
1 tsp Apple Pie Spice
1 tsp Baking Powder
½ cup shredded Coconut
2 cups Water

Instructions

Pour the water into the Instant Pot and lower the trivet. Grease a baking dish and set aside.

In a bowl, whisk together all the wet ingredients. In another, combine the dry ones. Gently whisk the mixtures together and pour into the greased dish. Place the dish on top of the trivet and put the lid on. Seal by turning clockwise. After the chime, select "MANUAL" and set the time for 40 minutes. Cook on HIGH.

When the timer goes off, press the "CANCEL" button. Move the handle to "Venting" to release the pressure quickly. When the pressure is fully released, open the lid. Remove the baking dish from the Instant Pot and let cool completely. Slice into 8 pieces.

Storing

Store the cake at room temperature in airtight container for 3-4 days. To freeze, divide among 8 Ziploc bags and place in the freezer. Consume within 3 months. Thaw in the fridge overnight and let reach room temperature.

Nutrition facts per serving

Calories 290, Protein 6g, Total Carbs 14g, Fat 23.5, Fiber 2g

Brownie Muffins

Preparation time: 15 minutes | Cooking time: 20 minutes | Servings: 6

Ingredients

1 Egg
¼ cup Slivered Almonds
¼ cup Caramel Syrup
1 tsp Apple Cider Vinegar
1 cup Flour
2 tbsp Butter, melted
¼ cup Cocoa Powder
1 tsp Vanilla Extract
½ cup Pumpkin Puree
½ tsp Salt
1 ½ cups Water

Instructions

Pour the water into the Instant Pot and lower the trivet. With an electric mixer, beat together all the ingredients until well combined. Divide the mixture between 6 silicone muffin cups. Place the muffins on top of the trivet. Put the lid on. Turn clockwise to seal. After the chime, press "MANUAL" and set the time to 20 minutes.

When the timer goes off, press the "CANCEL" button. Turn the pressure handle to "Venting" to release the pressure quickly. Open the lid and remove the muffin cups from the Instant Pot. Let cool completely.

Storing

Store in an airtight container at room temperature. To freeze, divide among 6 Ziploc bags and place in the freezer. Consume within 3 months. Thaw in the fridge overnight and let heat to room temperature to consume.

Nutrition facts per serving

Calories 280, Protein 7g, Total Carbs 22g, Fat 14g, Fiber 4g

Low Carb Cobbler with Blackberries

Preparation time: 15 minutes | Cooking time: 10 minutes | Servings: 2

Ingredients

2 tsp Heavy Cream
10 drops of Stevia
2 tsp Lemon Juice
¼ cup Coconut Flour
5 Egg Yolks
2 tbsp Coconut Oil
2 tbsp Erythritol
¼ tsp Baking Powder
¼ cup Blackberries
½ tsp Lemon Zest
Pinch of Salt
1 ½ cups Water

Instructions

Pour the water into the Instant Pot and lower the rack. Grease a baking dish and set aside. Whisk the yolks, heavy cream, lemon juice, coconut oil, stevia, salt, and erythritol. In another bowl, combine the dry ingredients.

Whisk the dry mixture into the wet one carefully, making sure there are no lumps. Fold in the blackberries. Pour the batter into the greased dish. Place on top of the trivet. Seal the lid by turning it clockwise and set the cooking mode to "MANUAL". Cook for 10 minutes.

When the timer goes off, press the "CANCEL" button. Move the handle to "Venting" to release the pressure quickly. When the pressure is fully released, open the lid. Remove the baking dish from the Instant Pot. Allow to cool completely.

Storing

Store in the fridge in an airtight container. Consume within 3 days. To freeze, divide among 2 Ziploc bags and place in the freezer. Consume within 3 months. Thaw in the fridge overnight.

Nutrition facts per serving

Calories 460, Protein 9g, Total Carbs 11g, Fat 44g, Fiber 6g

Cherry Clafoutis

Preparation time: 15 minutes | Cooking time: 25 minutes | Servings: 8

Ingredients

1 tbsp Vanilla
1 cup Milk
1 cup Flour
¼ cup Heavy Cream
1 ½ cups pitted and halved Cherries
⅓ cup Brown Sugar
¼ tsp Baking Soda
¼ tsp Baking Powder
1 ½ cups Water

Instructions

Pour the water into the Instant Pot and lower the trivet. Grease a baking dish with cooking spray and set aside.

Whisk together the eggs, milk, heavy cream, vanilla, and sugar. Gradually whisk in the rest of the ingredients, except the cherries. Pour the batter into the greased baking dish. Top with the cherries – skin side down – and place the baking dish on the trivet. Put the lid on and seal. Choose the "MANUAL" cooking mode and set the cooking time to 25 minutes. Cook on HIGH.

When the timer goes off, press the "CANCEL" button. To release the pressure quickly, turn the handle from "Sealing" to "Venting". When the pressure is fully released, open the lid. Remove the baking dish from the Instant Pot. Let cool before slicing.

Storing

Store at room temperature in airtight containers. To freeze, divide among Ziploc bags and place in the freezer. Consume within 3 months. Thaw in the fridge overnight and bring to room temperature before consuming.

Nutrition facts per serving

Calories 280, Protein 8g, Total Carbs 31g, Fat 11g, Fiber 2.5g

Gluten-Free Plantain Bread

Preparation time: 10 minutes | Cooking time: 40 minutes | Servings: 4

Ingredients

2 cups Almond Flour
3 tbsp Butter, melted
1 tbsp Vanilla Extract
2 Eggs, beaten
4 Plantains, mashed
1 tsp Baking Powder
Sugar to taste
1 ½ cups Water

Instructions

Pour the water into the Instant Pot and lower the trivet. Grease a loaf pan with cooking spray and set aside.

Place all the ingredients in a bowl and add sugar to taste. Check the taste and add more sugar if needed. Whisk everything together until the mixture is smooth.

Transfer the batter to the greased pan. Place the pan on top of the trivet and close the lid of the Instant Pot. To seal, turn clockwise. Choose "MANUAL" and set the time to 40 minutes. Cook on HIGH.

When the timer goes off, press the "CANCEL" button. Move the handle to "Venting" to release the pressure quickly. Open the lid and remove the pan from the Instant Pot. Allow to cool completely before slicing.

Storing

Store in an airtight container at room temperature. Consume for 3 days. To freeze, divide among four Ziploc bags and place in the freezer. Consume within 3 months. Thaw in the fridge overnight and bring to room temperature before consuming.

Nutrition facts per serving

Calories 180, Protein 2g, Total Carbs 35g, Fat 8, Fiber 5g

Stewed Coconut Butter Pears

Preparation time: 5 minutes | Cooking time: 10 minutes | Servings: 4

Ingredients

1 cup Water

¼ cup Sugar

2 tbsp Coconut Oil

3 tbsp Coconut Butter, melted

2 Large Pears, peeled and halved

¼ tsp Vanilla Extract

Instructions

Pour the water into the Instant Pot and lower the trivet. Place the pears in the steamer basket and lower into the pan. Put the lid on and seal by turning clockwise. After the chime, select "MANUAL" and cook for 2 minutes on HIGH.

After the beep, select the "CANCEL" button. Move the handle to "Venting" to release the pressure quickly.

When the pressure is fully released, open the lid and remove the pears from the Instant Pot. Discard the water from the Instant Pot and wipe it clean.

Add the remaining ingredients to the inner pot and set it to "SAUTE". Cook until melted. Add the pears and sauté for a few minutes, until sweet and glazed.

Storing

Store in Ziploc bags in the fridge and consume within 4 days. To freeze, divide among four Ziploc bags and place in the freezer. Consume within 3 months. Thaw in the fridge overnight.

Nutrition facts per serving

Calories 310, Protein 1g, Total Carbs 29g, Fat 19g, Fiber 5g

Plum Cake

Preparation time: 15 minutes | Cooking time: 25 minutes | Servings: 8

Ingredients

1 ½ cups Flour
2 tsp Baking Powder
½ cup Butter, softened
3 Eggs
¾ cup Milk
½ cup Coconut Flour
½ cup Sugar
4 Plums, pitted and halved
1 tsp Vanilla Extract
½ tsp Baking Powder
1 ½ cups Water

Instructions

Pour the water into the Instant Pot and lower the trivet. Grease a baking dish with cooking spray and set aside. Beat the butter and eggs with a mixer until creamy. Add the eggs and vanilla and beat until fluffy. Gradually beat in the milk. In a bowl, combine the dry ingredients.

Stir the dry mixture into the milk mixture. Pour into the baking dish and place the dish on the trivet. Put the lid of the Instant Pot on and turn clockwise to seal. Select the "MANUAL" cooking mode after the chime and set the cooking time to 25 minutes. Cook on HIGH.

After the beeping, select the "CANCEL" button. Move the handle to "Venting" to release the pressure quickly. When the pressure is fully released, open the lid and remove the baking dish from the Instant Pot. Allow to cool before slicing.

Storing

Store at room temperature in airtight containers. To freeze, divide among Ziploc bags and place in the freezer. Consume within 3 months. Thaw in the fridge overnight and bring to room temperature to consume.

Nutrition facts per serving

Calories 340 Protein 9g, Total Carbs 45g, Fat 25g, Fiber 1g

Sweet Almond Bread

Preparation time: 15 minutes | Cooking time: 30 minutes | Servings: 15

Ingredients

1 ½ cups Water
1 cup Flour
1 ½ cups Almond Flour
⅓ cup chopped Almonds
6 tbsp Butter, softened
6 tbsp Milk
¼ cup Protein Powder
½ tsp Baking Soda
2 tsp Baking Powder
4 Eggs
½ cup Oat Fiber
¼ cup Brown Sugar
2 tbsp Honey
6 ounces Yogurt

Instructions

Pour the water into the Instant Pot and lower the trivet. Grease a loaf pan with cooking spray and set aside.

Combine all the wet ingredients in one bowl. Whisk together the dry ones in another. Gently, whisk the two mixtures making sure not to leave any lumps.

Fold in the chopped almonds. Pour into the greased loaf pan and place the pan on top of the trivet.

Seal the lid by turning it clockwise and hit "MANUAL". With '+' and '-' set the time to 30 minutes. Cook on HIGH.

When the timer goes off, press the "CANCEL" button. Move the handle to "Venting" to release the pressure quickly.

When the pressure is fully released, open the lid. Remove the pan from the Instant Pot and let cool before slicing.

Storing

Store in airtight containers at room temperature. To freeze, divide among Ziploc bags and place in the freezer. Consume within 3 months. Thaw in the fridge overnight and bring to room temperature to consume.

Nutrition facts per serving

Calories 250, Protein 12g, Total Carbs 18g, Fat 12g, Fiber 5.5g

Strawberry Cream

Preparation time: 15 minutes | Cooking time: 2 minutes | Servings: 2

Ingredients

1 cup Strawberry Halves
1 cup Coconut Milk
2 tbsp Honey

Instructions

Whisk the milk and honey in the Instant Pot. Add the strawberries and put the lid on. Turn clockwise to seal. Select the "MANUAL" cooking mode after the chime and set the cooking time to 2 minutes. Cook on HIGH.

After the beeping sound, select the "CANCEL" button. Move the handle to "Venting" to release the pressure quickly. When the pressure is fully released, open the lid. Let cool completely.

Storing

Divide between glass jars, seal, and store in the fridge. Consume within 3 days. To freeze, divide among freezer cups with lids. Thaw in the fridge overnight and consume cold.

Nutrition facts per serving

Calories 120, Protein 1g, Total Carbs 16g, Fat 3g, Fiber 3g

Crunchy Peach and Coconut Dessert

Preparation time: 15 minutes | Cooking time: 4 minutes | Servings: 4

Ingredients

½ cup shredded Coconut

⅓ cup slivered Almonds

2 tbsp chopped Hazelnuts

½ cup Coconut Milk

3 Peaches, peeled and chopped

1 Pinch of Cinnamon

Instructions

Combine all the ingredients in your Instant Pot. Put the lid on and turn it clockwise to seal. When you hear the chime, press "MANUAL". Cook on HIGH for 4 minutes.

After the beeping, select the "CANCEL" button. Move the handle to "Venting" to release the pressure quickly. When the pressure is fully released, open the lid and allow to cool completely.

Storing

Store in the fridge in airtight containers and consume within 3 days. To freeze, divide between Ziploc bags, or freezer molds, and freeze for up to 3 months. Thaw overnight in the fridge and consume cold.

Nutrition facts per serving

Calories 150, Protein 4g, Total Carbs 11g, Fat 8g, Fiber 4g

21-DAY MEAL PLAN TO LOSE UP TO 20 POUNDS

Day	Breakfast	Lunch	Dinner	Dessert/ Snacks	Kkal
1	Mexican Salad	Lemongrass Drumsticks	Parmesan Risotto	Almond and Coconut Cake	1,540
2	Cinnamon Vanilla Oatmeal	Ham and Chicken White Penne	Chili Con Carne	Cherry Clafoutis	1,790
3	Chorizo Beans	Tomato and Kale Turkey	Beef Ribs and White Button Mushrooms	Plum Cake	1,715
4	Potato and Sausage Egg Pie	Dijon Meatloaf Ham and Chicken White Penne	Farro, Bean, and Mushroom Bake	Crunchy Peach and Coconut Dessert	1,743
5	Alfredo Pizza	Cheesy Prawn Casserole	Chili Braised Pork Chops	Parmesan-Crusted Potato Fries (x2)	1,720
6	Cheesy Almond Tuna Breakfast	Lentils and Beef + Mexican Salad	Tomato and Kale Turkey	Turmeric Sweet Potato Sticks (x2)	1,751
7	Mashed Potatoes with Sausage & Cheese	Chipotle Pork	Pesto Farfalle	Sweet Toasted Walnuts	1,780
8	Trout Salad Hard-Boiled Eggs	Garlicky Shredded Chicken	Ham and Chicken White Penne	Red Potatoes with Herbs	1,600
9	Chocolate Quinoa	Bean & Pork Stew + Farro, Bean, and Mushroom Bake	Green Olives and Onion Chicken	Banana Almond Butter Healthy Bars (x2)	1,519
10	Bacon and Feta Couscous	Gorgonzola Beef Medley with Cabbage	Spaghetti Bolognese + Tuna Melt	Almond and Coconut Cake	1,670
11	Beet Borscht + Chorizo Beans	Chicken, Bean, and Tomato Bake	Sage Pork with Yams	Baba Ghanoush + Strawberry Cream	1,565

12	Mini Bacon Quiches	Paleo Stuffed Peppers	Sweet Cumin and Ginger Chicken	'Fried' Cinnamon Banana	1,596
13	Cheesy Almond Tuna Breakfast	Peanut Chicken Noodles	Lentils and Beef	Low Carb Cobbler with Blackberries	1,652
14	Fruity Pecan Breakfast Cobbler	Mexican Salad	Simple Buttery Pork Chops	Gluten-Free Plantain Bread	1,604
15	Hard-Boiled Eggs + Bacon and Feta Couscous	Beef Cubes with Zucchini and Tomatoes + Chili Braised Pork Chops	Chicken, Bean, and Tomato Bake	Strawberry Cream	1,690
16	Mexican Salad	Sweet Cumin and Ginger Chicken	Paleo Stuffed Peppers	Prosciutto-Dressed Asparagus	1,736
17	Brie and Bacon Frittata	Sage Pork with Yams + Beet Borscht	Mexican-Spiced Chicken + Baba Ghanoush	Tuna Melt (x2)	1,670
18	Breakfast Ham Grits	Scotch Eggs + Trout Salad	Red Bean Patties	Stewed Coconut Butter Pears	1,600
19	Chorizo Beans	Creamy Mushroom Pasta	Tomato and Kale Turkey	Crab Bites (x2)	1,560
20	Sausage, Spinach, and Onion Casserole	Tomato Beef Brisket	Cheesy Asparagus Pasta	Cherry Clafoutis	1,595
21	Mexican Breakfast Casserole	Enchilada Chicken Casserole with Cauliflower	Bean & Pork Stew + Parmesan Risotto	Plum Cake	1,701

63079344R00062

Made in the USA
Middletown, DE
25 August 2019